The Irish In America

Immigration, Land, Probate, Administrations, Birth,
Marriage and Burial Records of the Irish
in America in and about the
Eighteenth Century

I0117123

By MICHAEL J. O'BRIEN

Excerpted from

THE JOURNAL OF THE AMERICAN IRISH
HISTORICAL SOCIETY

CLEARFIELD

Originally Published
New York, 1914

Excerpted and Reprinted from
The Journal of the American Irish Historical Society,
Volume XIII, 1914
Genealogical Publishing Co., Inc.
Baltimore, 1965

Reissued
Genealogical Publishing Co., Inc.
Baltimore, 1974

Reprinted for
Clearfield Company, Inc. by
Genealogical Publishing Co., Inc.
Baltimore, Maryland
1990, 1993, 1996, 2002

Library of Congress Catalogue Card Number 65-29278
International Standard Book Number: 0-8063-0603-3

Made in the United States of America

TABLE OF CONTENTS

IMMIGRATION, LAND, PROBATE, ADMINISTRATION, BIRTH, MARRIAGE AND BURIAL RECORDS OF THE IRISH IN AMERICA IN AND ABOUT THE EIGHTEENTH CENTURY.

BY MICHAEL J. O'BRIEN.

VITAL RECORDS OF GEORGETOWN, ME.

COPIED BY MICHAEL J. O'BRIEN.

Children.	Date of Birth.			Parents.
Ann	Jan.	17,	1739	William and Martha Butler
Martha	May	28,	1742	William and Martha Butler
Sarah	Jan.	27,	1744	William and Martha Butler
William	Nov.	25,	1746	William and Martha Butler
Abigail	March	15,	1750	William and Martha Butler
Thomas	Feb.	18,	1754	William and Martha Butler
William	April	22,	1780	Thomas and Margaret Butler
George	July	6,	1782	Thomas and Margaret Butler
Thomas	June	17,	1784	Thomas and Margaret Butler
Abigail	Oct.	26,	1786	Thomas and Margaret Butler
John	March	31,	1788	Thomas and Margaret Butler
James	Nov.	29,	1790	Thomas and Margaret Butler
Anna	Dec.	31,	1794	Thomas and Margaret Butler
Martha	Dec.	13,	1797	Thomas and Margaret Butler
Margaret	Oct.	5,	1801	Thomas and Margaret Butler
Martha	May	5,	1755	William and Jane Cummings
William	Jan.	26,	1747	James and Isabella Cunningham
Jane	Feb.	3,	1749	James and Isabella Cunningham
John	March	16,	1751	James and Isabella Cunningham
Jane	Oct.	7,	1750	John and Jane Clarey
John	June	10,	1753	John and Jane Clarey
Allen	June	8,	1756	John and Jane Clarey
Robert	April	10,	1759	John and Jane Clarey
Ruth	April	10,	1759	John and Jane Clarey
John	Sept.	12,	1780	Allen and Mary Clarey
Nancy	Feb.	20,	1783	Allen and Mary Clarey
Allen	April	2,	1786	Allen and Mary Clarey
David	Dec.	8,	1789	Allen and Mary Clarey
James	July	21,	1791	Allen and Mary Clarey
Edward	Feb.	11,	1794	Allen and Mary Clarey
Robert	Aug.	14,	1796	Allen and Mary Clarey
Mary	Sept.	5,	1800	Allen and Mary Clarey

Children.	Date of Birth.	Parents.
Samuel	Dec. 27, 1789	Jeremiah and Eliza Connell
Margaret	Aug. 23, 1745	—— and Margaret Carty
John	Jan. 28, 1789	William and Katherine Coffee
William	Sept. 5, 1790	William and Katherine Coffee
Elisha	Nov. 10, 1798	Patrick and Dorcas Connelly
Andrew	July 4, 1800	Patrick and Dorcas Connelly
George	Aug. 14, 1801	Patrick and Dorcas Connelly
James R.	April 2, 1799	Isiah and Hannah Corbett
Nancy	June 4, 1800	Isiah and Hannah Corbett
Robert	Jan. 16, 1802	Isiah and Hannah Corbett
David	May 29, 1798	Peter and Nancy Carey
Samuel	June 12, 1800	Peter and Nancy Carey
Sally	June 12, 1800	Peter and Nancy Carey
Robert	Sept. 22, 1790	Patrick and Mercy Drummond
Jacob	Feb. 17, 1792	Patrick and Mercy Drummond
Alexander	April 1, 1794	Patrick and Mercy Drummond
Jane	April 1, 1794	Patrick and Mercy Drummond
Jane	July 22, 1741	Patrick and Susannah Drummond
John	Sept. 22, 1744	Patrick and Susannah Drummond
Mary	Nov. 4, 1747	Patrick and Susannah Drummond
Katherine	Nov. 8, 1749	Patrick and Susannah Drummond
Settessha	April 8, 1753	Patrick and Susannah Drummond
Ann	July 6, 1755	Patrick and Susannah Drummond
Margaret	May 1, 1733	James and Catrina Drummond
Alexander	May 1, 1736	James and Catrina Drummond
James	May —, 1739	James and Catrina Drummond
Mary	Oct. 30, 1756	Thomas and Dorcas Donnell
Sarah	Jan. 27, 1758	Thomas and Dorcas Donnell
Sarah	March 12, 1741	John and Mary Fling
Ann	July 15, 1741	William and Jane Grace
Jane	Oct. 12, 1739	David and Mary Gilmore
David	Oct. 6, 1743	David and Mary Gilmore
James	Feb. 1, 1788	John and Bashaby Gahan
Peggy	Feb. 2, 1790	John and Bashaby Gahan
John	Dec. 23, 1792	John and Bashaby Gahan
Jeremiah	Sept. 17, 1794	John and Bashaby Gahan
Sarah	Dec. 26, 1796	John and Bashaby Gahan
William Butler	July 10, 1799	John and Bashaby Gahan
Samuel Webb	Feb. 6, 1803	John and Bashaby Gahan
Rachel	Feb. 22, 1790	James and Betsey Gahan
James	Jan. 10, 1792	James and Betsey Gahan
Patrick	Feb. 26, 1794	James and Betsey Gahan
William	April 22, 1795	James and Betsey Gahan
Dennis	Jan. 29, 1798	James and Betsey Gahan
James	Nov. 20, 1755	Thomas and Mary Higgens
Hannah	March 20, 1758	Thomas and Mary Higgens

Children.	Date of Birth.			Parents.
Priscilla	May	30,	1764	Joseph and Experience Higgens
Joseph	June	23,	1766	Joseph and Experience Higgens
Jonathan	March	17,	1768	Joseph and Experience Higgens
Eleanor	Sept.	17,	1772	James Hogan and wife
Thomas	Aug.	9,	1774	James Hogan and wife
Jean	Oct.	1,	1776	James Hogan and wife
Margaret	Nov.	28,	1778	James Hogan and wife
James	Nov.	29,	1780	James Hogan and wife
William	Nov.	9,	1782	James Hogan and wife
Nancy	Aug.	5,	1776	Thomas Hogan and wife
Mary	May	29,	1786	Thomas Hogan and wife
Michael	Feb.	29,	1788	Thomas Hogan and wife
Edmund	May	14,	1790	Thomas Hogan and wife
Nicholas	Aug.	25,	1776	Thomas Hogan and wife
Margaret	June	1,	1781	Thomas Hogan and wife
John	Dec.	1,	1784	Thomas Hogan and wife
Andrew	May	30,	1791	Thomas Hogan and wife
Polly	Nov.	30,	1782	Thomas Hogan and wife
James	June	29,	1793	Thomas Hogan and wife
William	June	29,	1793	Thomas Hogan and wife
Catherine	Jan.	6,	1798	Thomas Hogan and wife
Hannah	May	9,	1798	Richard and Jane Hogan
Nancy	May	10,	1799	Nicholas and Eleanor Hogan
Elizabeth	Sept.	24,	1801	Nicholas and Eleanor Hogan
William	Sept.	20,	1800	Nicholas and Eleanor Hogan
Eliza	Sept.	26,	1802	Nicholas and Eleanor Hogan
Susanna	Oct.	19,	1804	Nicholas and Eleanor Hogan
Margaret	Jan.	10,	1806	Nicholas and Eleanor Hogan
Thomas	April	16,	1808	Nicholas and Eleanor Hogan
Thomas	Sept.	25,	1780	James and Sarah Hogan
Polly	Jan.	16,	1785	James and Sarah Hogan
Hannah	July	14,	1788	James and Sarah Hogan
Thomas	May	12,	1790	James and Sarah Hogan
Samuel	Jan.	17,	1801	Andrew and Eliza Herrin
Catherine	Feb.	17,	1780	John and Mary Kelly
Anna	April	29,	1782	John and Mary Kelly
John	Oct.	16,	1786	John and Mary Kelly
Thomas	Oct.	13,	1788	John and Mary Kelly
Mary	Nov.	11,	1792	John and Mary Kelly
John	Sept.	14,	1751	William and Catherine Kelley
John	May	31,	1729	James and Rebecca McFadden
Mary	July	9,	1731	James and Rebecca McFadden
James	Nov.	2,	1733	James and Rebecca McFadden
Hannah	Feb.	22,	1736	James and Rebecca McFadden
Thomas	Oct.	17,	1740	James and Rebecca McFadden
Andrew	Jan.	3,	1742	James and Rebecca McFadden

Children.	*Date of Birth.*			*Parents.*
Jane	Oct.	13,	1748	James and Rebecca McFadden
Jane	Dec.	12,	1743	Daniel and Margaret McFadden
Mary	Aug.	4,	1745	Daniel and Margaret McFadden
James	Sept.	24,	1749	Daniel and Margaret McFadden
Daniel	Jan.	5,	1751	Daniel and Margaret McFadden
Margaret	March	3,	1753	Daniel and Margaret McFadden
John	March	9,	1757	Daniel and Margaret McFadden
Elizabeth	March	21,	1760	Daniel and Margaret McFadden
Thomas	Oct.	1,	1762	Daniel and Margaret McFadden
William	May	22,	1751	Andrew and Abigail McFadden
Martha	July	17,	1752	Andrew and Abigail McFadden
Jane	Sept.	13,	1754	Andrew and Abigail McFadden
Andrew	Aug.	5,	1757	Andrew and Abigail McFadden
Abigail	Aug.	5,	1757	Andrew and Abigail McFadden
John	March	3,	1762	Andrew and Abigail McFadden
Rachel	Nov.	26,	1778	John and Patience McFadden
Letis	Aug.	16,	1782	John and Patience McFadden
Robert	Feb.	19,	1788	John and Patience McFadden
Margaret	April	20,	1794	John and Patience McFadden
Rebecca	Oct.	7,	1768	Thomas and Hannah McFadden
Molly	Aug.	28,	1770	Thomas and Hannah McFadden
Peggy	Dec.	18,	1780	Daniel and Jane McFadden
Nancy	Aug.	30,	1782	Daniel and Jane McFadden
Susannah	Oct.	29,	1775	James and Lettis McFadden
Daniel	June	11,	1778	James and Lettis McFadden
Lettise	Sept.	24,	1785	James and Mary McFadden
Thomas	Feb.	13,	1787	James and Mary McFadden
Samuel	March	13,	1789	James and Mary McFadden
James	Oct.	24,	1793	James and Mary McFadden
David	May	25,	1795	James and Mary McFadden
Nancy	Oct.	26,	1796	James and Mary McFadden
John	March	21,	1799	James and Mary McFadden
Martha	Nov.	3,	1793	John and Mary McFadden
John	June	8,	1795	John and Mary McFadden
Nancy	July	7,	1797	John and Mary McFadden
Betsey	June	20,	1799	John and Mary McFadden
Andrew	Sept.	5,	1801	John and Mary McFadden
Mary	Aug.	31,	1804	John and Mary McFadden
Julia Ann	Oct.	3,	1806	John and Mary McFadden
John	Dec.	17,	1744	Patrick and Jane Mahoney
James	Nov.	25,	1747	Patrick and Jane Mahoney
Patrick	March	10,	1749	Patrick and Jane Mahoney
Lucy	Feb.	14,	1771	James and Abigail Mahoney
James	Feb.	12,	1773	James and Abigail Mahoney
Ruth	Feb.	11,	1775	James and Abigail Mahoney
John	May	24,	1777	James and Abigail Mahoney

Children.	Date of Birth.			Parents.
Patrick	July	12,	1779	James and Abigail Mahoney
Abigail	Feb.	19,	1781	James and Abigail Mahoney
Phebe	Aug.	21,	1783	James and Abigail Mahoney
Peggy	Jan.	16,	1787	James and Abigail Mahoney
Thomas	Jan.	14,	1790	James and Abigail Mahoney
Charles	Aug.	24,	1792	James and Abigail Mahoney
Thomas	Feb.	20,	1796	James and Abigail Mahoney
Nancy	March	15,	1796	James and Martha Mahoney
Osgood	June	25,	1798	James and Martha Mahoney
Rebecca	March	28,	1755	Mathew and Hannah McKenny
Jane	Feb.	21,	1756	Mathew and Hannah McKenny
Betsey	May	29,	1767	Mathew and Hannah McKenny
Thomas	——			Mathew and Hannah McKenny
Mary	——			Mathew and Hannah McKenny
John	——			Mathew and Hannah McKenny
James	Feb.	28,	1773	Mathew and Hannah McKenny
Lucy	Sept.	14,	1774	Mathew and Hannah McKenny
Mathew	——			Mathew and Hannah McKenny
Benjamin	Oct.	17,	1778	Mathew and Hannah McKenny
Andrew	——			Mathew and Hannah McKenny
Ebenezer	April	15,	1786	Mathew and Hannah McKenny
Mary	Aug.	23,	1746	Mathew and Mary McKenny
Benjamin	May	11,	1749	Mathew and Mary McKenny
Abigail	Feb.	28,	1753	George and Sarah McKenny
Mary	March	17,	1755	George and Sarah McKenny
Robert	April	17,	1758	George and Sarah McKenny
Andrew	Nov.	16,	1760	George and Sarah McKenny
Thomas	June	15,	1765	Brooks and Abigail McKenny
Betsey	May	29,	1767	Brooks and Abigail McKenny
Rachel	Oct.	3,	1769	Brooks and Abigail McKenny
Brooks	Feb.	7,	1772	Brooks and Abigail McKenny
Fanny	July	24,	1774	Brooks and Abigail McKenny
George	Aug.	12,	1776	Brooks and Abigail McKenny
Molly	Nov.	1,	1778	Brooks and Abigail McKenny
Abigail	March	1,	1781	Brooks and Abigail McKenny
Mathew	Jan.	2,	1784	Brooks and Abigail McKenny
Anna	Dec.	19,	1786	Brooks and Abigail McKenny
Deborah	June	14,	1788	Brooks and Abigail McKenny
Hannah	March	17,	1740	Terrence and Elizabeth McMahon
Mickael	July	20,	1743	Terrence and Elizabeth McMahon
Nathaniel	Feb.	10,	1745	Terrence and Elizabeth McMabon
Terrance	Sept.	21,	1747	Terrence and Elizabeth McMahon
Joseph	June	27,	1750	Terrence and Elizabeth McMahon
Ann Holerin	Feb.	28,	1753	Terrence and Elizabeth McMahon
Elizabeth Donnell	March	29,	1756	Terrence and Elizabeth McMahon
Timothy	May	21,	1762	Terrence and Elizabeth McMahon

Children.	Date of Birth.			Parents.
Thomas	May	21,	1762	Terrence and Elizabeth McMahon
Almira	April	24,	1789	Timothy and Mary McMahon
John	April	19,	1791	Timothy and Mary McMahon
Mary	Dec.	20,	1778	Daniel and Sarah McMahon
Patty	Sept.	23,	1781	Daniel and Sarah McMahon
Dorcas	Aug.	11,	1787	Daniel and Sarah McMahon
Thomas Donnell	Aug.	25,	1790	Daniel and Sarah McMahon
Eliza Donnell	Sept.	1,	1793	Daniel and Sarah McMahon
Daniel	Aug.	14,	1762	Michael and Eunice Mahan
Molly	Oct.	11,	1770	James and Sarah Murphy
James	Jan.	2,	1767	James and Sarah McHonane
Elizabeth	Oct.	25,	1768	James and Sarah McHonane
Sarah	Aug.	21,	1771	James and Sarah McHonane
Ann	Aug.	4,	1773	James and Sarah McHonane
John	Aug.	26,	1778	Timothy and Catherine McCarty
Mary	Sept.	23,	1780	Timothy and Catherine McCarty
Thomas	Nov.	23,	1782	Timothy and Catherine McCarty
Collins	Dec.	8,	1784	Timothy and Catherine McCarty
Brian	Jan.	22,	1786	Timothy and Catherine McCarty
Collins	March	24,	1788	Timothy and Catherine McCarty
Samuel	May	4,	1790	Timothy and Catherine McCarty
Catherine	Sept.	13,	1792	Timothy and Catherine McCarty
James	March	13,	1795	Timothy and Catherine McCarty
Eleanor	March	13,	1796	Timothy and Catherine McCarty
Betsey	Aug.	16,	1798	Timothy and Catherine McCarty
Sarah	Oct.	23,	1803	Timothy and Catherine McCarty
Betsey	March	18,	1788	John and Betsey O'Dee
Mary	March	1,	1755	John and Lucretia Quinn
Margaret	Oct.	6,	1756	John and Lucretia Quinn
James	Feb.	1,	1758	John and Lucretia Quinn
John	Feb.	1,	1760	John and Lucretia Quinn
John	June	30,	1764	John and Lucretia Quinn
Catherine	July	19,	1749	Timothy and Margaret Roarke
John	Nov.	30,	1750	Timothy and Margaret Roarke
Mary	April	7,	1745	John and Isabella Sullivan
John	Aug.	10,	1746	John and Isabella Sullivan
Jane	Mar.	11,	1747	John and Isabella Sullivan
William	April	5,	1750	John and Isabella Sullivan
Elizabeth	Sept.	28,	1791	Daniel and Elizabeth Sullivan
Catherine	April	17,	1767	William and Mary Shanahorn
William	Nov.	17,	1768	William and Mary Shanahorn
Eleanor	Jan.	26,	1778	Michael and Eleanor Shea
Nancy	Sept.	22,	1780	Michael and Eleanor Shea
Jane	Jan.	31,	1782	Michael and Eleanor Shea
Pierce	May	1,	1784	Michael and Eleanor Shea
John	Feb.	7,	1787	Michael and Eleanor Shea

Children.	Date of Birth.		Parents.
Thomas	July	6, 1788	Michael and Eleanor Shea
Philip	March	26, 1790	Michael and Eleanor Shea
Nicholas	Feb.	18, 1782	Philip and Eliza Shea
David	June	19, 1795	Philip and Eliza Shea
James	Aug.	12, 1736	Patrick and Mary Work
John	Oct.	19, 1738	Patrick and Mary Work
Daniel	Nov.	28, 1743	Patrick and Mary Work
Patrick	March	28, 1746	Patrick and Mary Work
Andrew	Oct.	19, 1748	Patrick and Mary Work
David	Jan.	5, 1751	Patrick and Mary Work
Mary	Oct.	25, 1753	Patrick and Mary Work
Ephraim	Feb.	21, 1756	Patrick and Mary. Work.

IRISH IMMIGRANTS TO NEW ENGLAND—EXTRACTS FROM THE MINUTES OF THE SELECTMEN OF THE TOWN OF BOSTON, MASS.

BY MICHAEL J. O'BRIEN

In the years 1635 and 1636 many ships came to New England from English, Irish and Welsh ports. One of them, the *Saint Patrick*, Captain Palmer, which arrived at Boston from Ireland on May 15, 1636, was a noted vessel of the time and is mentioned by Governor Winthrop in his much quoted Journal. It is related that when the Irish ship came into Boston Harbor "a great stir was made because of the failure of her captain to salute the English flag on Castle Island." The lieutenant of the fort boarded the vessel, and, as we are told, "made her strike her flag." Captain Palmer complained of this to Governor Winthrop, who required the lieutenant "to acknowledge his error lest the lord deputy of Ireland (Wentworth) should be informed."—(*Vide* New York Genealogical and Biographical Record, Vol. 10, page 150.)

Governor Winthrop was educated at Trinity College, Dublin, and is said to have entertained friendly feelings toward Ireland. Sir Thomas Wentworth (afterwards lord lieutenant), in co-operation with the governor, sought to plant colonies of Irish people in New England as an offset to the influence of the Puritans, whom he despised. In this they were not very successful, although it is known they did induce several Irish families to come to the colony, and I have no doubt that some of the Irish names which I have found at various times when examining the copies of the earliest New England records, as published by the historical societies, were those of the people shipped out of Ireland by Lord Wentworth, or perhaps, were their descendants.

The Winthrops were an English family, but I find, on examining their genealogy, that several of them settled in the south of Ireland late in the sixteenth century. The genealogy indicates that the family remained permanently in Ireland and has had many branches there. One of them located on lands at Aghadowne, County Cork, and two others on estates near Bandon. In the Winthrop Papers at Boston there are references to communications passing between the Irish and New England branches. Among them is a letter from the widow of Adam Winthrop, the Governor's cousin, dated "Bandon Bridge in Ireland, March 5, 1637," informing the governor of the death of her husband and asking for financial aid. There is another letter, dated "Cork, February 25, 1696," and still another, dated "Baltimore (County Cork) June 9, 1698," from one of the Irish branch addressed to Waite Winthrop, then one of the judges of the court at Boston.

The "Minutes of the Selectmen of the Town of Boston," as published by the Board of Record Commissioners of that City, contain numerous references to the Irish who entered the colony through that port. I have made a very thorough examination of the "Minutes" and have extracted from them much information that is of interest to Americans of Irish blood. It is clear from these records that Irish immigrants came to New England through the port of Boston in great numbers and that the exodus from Ireland continued all through the eighteenth century. For the purpose of the present paper, I have selected references to the ships which registered at Boston as from Irish ports between the years 1716 and 1769. The names of the passengers are not given in all cases, but, where they are mentioned, they indicated a good percentage of names of old Irish origin.

SOME REFERENCES TO THE ARRIVAL, AT THE PORT OF
BOSTON, OF PASSENGER-CARRYING SHIPS FROM IRISH
PORTS, COPIED FROM "THE MINUTES OF THE SELECT-
MEN OF THE TOWN OF BOSTON."

Ships *Truth* and *Daylight* arrived "from Ireland" May 21,
1716.

Ship *Mary Ann*, "from Dublin," arrived June 16, 1716.

Ship *Globe*, "from Ireland," arrived June 25, 1716. She had
twenty-nine passengers, among them: Charles O'Hara, shoemaker; James Hines, shoemaker; John Ennis, currier; Elizabeth
Doyle, cook; Patrick Fargison, mariner.

The ships *Patience* and *Judith* arrived "from London" June
30, 1716. Among her passengers were John Fitzgerald, Patrick
Ogilvie and John Brandon.

The ship *America* arrived "from Lisburn in Ireland," July 3,
1716.

At a meeting of the Selectmen held on August 12, 1718, it
was "Voted that Mr. John Marion be impowered on behalfe of
the sd. Sel men to appear before the Court of Genll Sessions of
the Peace for the County of Suffolk at their present Sessions to
move what he Shall think proper in order to Secure this Town
from Charges whch may hapen to accrue or be imposed on them
by reason of the Passengers Lately Arived here from Ireland or
elsewhere."

At a meeting on September 12, 1724, Captain Philip Bass was
called before the selectmen, "it appearing that he had the Measles
(an Infectious Sickness) among his Passengers in his vessel lately
come from Ireland into this Harbour. The said Philip Bass was
ordered forthwith to Cause his Said vessel to go down near Spectacle Island with what Passengers and goods he has on Board,
etc."

At a meeting on August 16, 1736, Captain Benedict Arnold
appeared and gave information that "he came from Ireland
about twelve weeks ago and that he is bound for Philadelphia
with his passengers, who in all are 120. Hopes to sail in a few
days as soon as he can recruit with water and Provissions and
promises that the Passengers which came as have yesterday
shall repair on board again to-day. The ship's name is the *Pru-
dent Hannah*."

At a meeting on August 9, 1736, mention is made of "19 Transports just imported from Cork in Ireland." The master of the vessel, on being sent for, promised "to take proper care of the Passengers and would see they would not come ashore. Was on his way to Virginia, whither he intended to sail in 8 or 10 days."

Meeting of September 22, 1736. The following persons were reported as having been brought from Ireland by Captain John Carrell:

George Lucas, wife and children
Honora Cinae, wife of Dinish Cinae
James and peter Cinae, and their children.

Elizabeth Lamb	Agnes Proctor
Sally Lamb	Mary Burton
Betty Lamb	Thomas Howard
Nancy Lamb	Dennis Kenny
Nellie Lamb	William Steward
Beckee Lamb	

The Selectmen admitted all as "Inhabitants."

Meeting on November 10, 1736. "Captain George Beard, present, Executed a Bond on his part of the Penalty of One Thousand Pounds to Indemnify the Town from Charges on Account of Thirty Seven Passengers Imported by him from Ireland in the Sloop *Hannah*."

Meeting of November 26, 1736. "Captain James Williams together with Gershom Keyes and Josiah Flagg gave Bond of the Penalty of Eleven Hundred Pounds to Indemnify the Town from any Charge on Account of Forty Three Passengers by the said Williams Imported from Ireland in the Sloop *Two Mollys*."

June 24, 1737. In a list of passengers who came in the ship *Catherine* from Ireland, Bryan Karrick and Catherine Driscoll are mentioned. Mr. Thomas Gunter, merchant, gave bond on their behalf.

September 7, 1737. Captain Daniel Gibbs, "Commander of the Ship *Sagamore* from Ireland," was called before the meeting to report upon the condition of the passengers who were reported to be "sick with the Measels." He was directed to take his ship and passengers to Spectacle Island "in Order to their Airing themselves and their Bedding Clothes and to Continue there until further Order." Captain Gibbs again appeared on September 14, 1737, when a certificate was issued to him permitting the passengers "to come up to this Town." There were twenty-seven people on board the *Sagamore*.

September 15, 1737. Mr. Samuel Todd appeared and offered to give bond "for Passengers from Ireland in the Brigantine *Elizabeth*." The bond was accepted for £500.

November 8, 1737. "Captain James Finney, John Karr and William Hall Executed a Bond of the Penalty of Six Hundred Pounds to Indemnify the Town on Account of One Hundred and Sixty two Passengers Imported by the said Finney in the Snow *Charming Molly* from Ireland, November 7th, 1737."

December 13, 1738. "Captain Nathaniel Montgomery gave Bond for Five Hundred Pounds on Account 82 Passengers imported in the *Eagle*, William Acton, Master, from Ireland."

May 29, 1739. Captain Ephraim Jackson, Commander of the ship *Barwick*, gave bond for £250 "to Indemnify the Town on Account 46 Passengers imported in the ship *Barwick* from Ireland."

October 7, 1741. Captains John Seymour and William Palmer were notified "to Appear and give Bonds to the Town Treasurer for the Passengers they have Imported from Ireland."

At the meeting held on October 31, 1741, a long report on the condition of the passengers on the sloop *Seaflower* from Belfast was read. She sailed from Belfast on July 10, 1741, with 106 passengers and arrived at Boston on October 31, having lost her captain and forty of the passengers "through hunger and want of provisions." The remaining passengers were reduced to a frightful condition of starvation and would have perished but for being rescued by a man-of-war, which brought them into Boston. They were bound for Philadelphia. The selectmen ordered them to be taken to the almshouse and provided with nourishment and medicines.

August 19, 1744: "The Selectmen sent up to the Almshouse Sixteen Girls and Three Boys and a Woman arrived here yesterday from Cape Breton who were taken About Six Weeks since by a French Privateer, being bound from Ireland to Philadelphia." The overseer of the poor was directed to maintain them "at the expense of the Province." Their names were:

James Conner
Thomas Bryan
Charles White
Mary Roberts
Mary White
Sarah Agin
Mary Benson
Margaret Anderson
Fanny Brady
Katharine Morris

Sarah Kathary
Elizabeth Campbell
Mary Hammond
Eliza Fitzgerald
Sarah Mchun
Bridget McNamarra
Eliza Dunster
Jenny Richardson
Mary Derham

May 21, 1763. "Captain Daniel Maccarthy, Master of the ship *Sally* from Kinsale in Ireland, upon Examination declares that he left said place the 23rd. March and this day arrived at Nantasket Road," etc. The mate of the vessel died on the voyage and the captain was compelled to certify that he had destroyed his clothing and effects before his passengers would be allowed to land.

May 21, 1764. "William Clouston, Master of the Brigantine *Hound*, appeared and reported that he has been from Cork in Ireland 34 days."

November 16, 1768. The Surgeon's Mate of the *Robert* appeared and reported the arrival of the ship from Cork in Ireland and the condition of his passengers.

PORT ARRIVALS—IMMIGRANTS.

Under this head a large number of Irish names appear in the Town Books of Boston, beginning with the year 1762 and down to 1769. There is no other information regarding these immigrants, except that, in some instances, they came in ships from Irish ports and in many cases their occupations are given as farmers, artisans, mariners, laborers or servants.

Arrivals in Year 1762.

"John Poor from Iarland, bookkeeper."
John Casey
William Shannon
Edward Shaahay

Patrick Power
Richard Power
Thomas Power
David Dunn
Patrick Phealan

Michael Nevil
Thomas Gleason
John Clary

1763.

Patrick Poor
John Roach
Morris Dunlay
John Dunlay
Hugh McCoy
John McKean
John Molony
James Carrol
Catharine Ceasey
William Dougharty
Henry Clarey
Thomas Cain
James Fitzpatrick
Michael McCarney
Margaret Quark
Jane Kelly
William Kelley
Francis Murphy
Patrick White

Patrick Dumphey
Edward Morrosey
Catherine Corkran
Thomas Casey
Lydia Ryan
Michael Colman
John Dillon
Mrs. Melone
Daniel Kenney
William McGrath
Ann Moore
Peter Doyle
——— Gilroy
Ralph O'Donal
John Doughny
Patrick Drohan
Simon Hannahan
Richard Welsh
James Roach

Patrick Felleter
Richard Fleming
Christopher Collins
Patrick Power
Patrick Shallow
Thomas Murphey
William Murphey
Lewis Fitch Gerrald
John Delaney
John Tobing
Philip Stapleton
James Nowling
Michael Fling
Michael Keeting
Christopher Barret
Patrick Killey
James Kennedy
"Mr. O'Neal, a Trader"

1764.

John Mackdonel
John Whealden
William Larken
Thomas Larken
Dr. Kannady & family
Catherine O'Donely
Onner Soloven
John Carton
Michael Claire

Charles Riney
Catherine Riney
Cornelius Obruin
John Cotter
John Kelly
William Logan
William Gillmore
James Shannon
John Timmins

Richard Gallispie
John Kennedy
James Coghran
Daniel Dockery
Patrick McClaran
Patrick McCowan
Patrick Laply
John Burk

On the schooner *Hannah*, which arrived September 11, from Cork, there were:

Francis Rien
James Coffe
James Brien
Mrs. Dorin
Morgan Mullons
Mary Connell
John Costolo

James Furlong
James Stewart
Benjamin Davison
John Callahan (1)
John Callahan (2)
John Branfield
Patrick Harden

John Reding
Richard Bourke
Michael Clary
Timothy Collens
John Bryen
James Ryon
Capt. ——— Cavenough

The brig *Freemason*, which arrived from Cork on December 27, brought:

Richard Burk
John Roberts
Matthew McNamara
David Howe
Malaky Field
John Cleary

John Brown
Edward Moor
John Moor
Martin Dunavan
William Dunavan
Mary Dunavan

Mary Dresden
John Lyon
Andrew Barrett
Catherine Lynch

Arrivals in 1765.

John Kavanaugh
John Murphy
Patrick Dallaney
Thomas Ring
Michael McNamara
John McGrah
Cornelius Mahan
Luke Shannon
John Sullivan and wife
Michael Flanegin
Philip Ryan
John Ryan
Thomas Glody
Edmond Magrath
John Cuff
Hugh Keen
Thomas Fitzgearld
Patrick Kerrel
Elizabeth Wall
John McDaniel
Robert Carrel
Thomas Collins
John McCannon
Christopher Kennedy
John Duggin
Juda Duggin
John Kelley
Elizabeth Murphy

Peter Ryan
John Herrington
Patrick Conner
Valentine Conner
Dennis Roian
Patrick Dowling
Peter Doyle
John Fling
James Ryan
Daniel Moore
Richard Kelley
Jeremiah Daley
James Flood
John Logen
Michael McNemaro
——— McCarty
Con. Casey
Timothy Cotterill
John Gilroy
William Hannon
Patrick Dutting
Patrick Nuff
Jeremiah Haley
William Carey
Thomas Keefe
Edmond Barret
John Ryan
Davis Welch

John Shannahan
Patrick Herrin
Thomas Keoho
Thomas Linch
Moses Roach
William Cummins
John Larey
John Bryan
John Burk
John Cunningham
Thomas Roach
Cornelius Nophen
Matthew Kelley
John Flannigan
John Callahan
William Doyde
John Pendergrass
Michael Carney
Morris Garey
Jeremiah Folley
George Fitzpatrick
John McGee
Charles Dorren
Richard Luby
David Sullivan
Joseph Quin

1766.

Patrick Mahon
John McCarter
John Canby
Charles Comerin
John Brinnon
James Doyle
Henry McKennery
Patrick Campbell
William Boyde

William Higgings
Michael Bryan
Timothy Conner
Peter Larey
Michael Neal
James Toole
Thomas Gibbens
Patrick Dowling
Edward Whealand

Peter Hogan
Patrick "Naster"
Patrick Furnas
Edward Casey
Darby Morrison
Martin McLartin
Edward Butler
John Killey

The brig *William* from Ireland, which arrived September 29, had sixty passengers:

Mr. Barry, schoolmaster
William Scott, school-
    master and wife
Timothy Dorson, school-
    master, and wife
William Moor
Daniel Boyles and wife
Michael Poor
John Feald
Jeremiah Nuhan
Timothy Shea
William Gorman
Jeremiah Reardon
John Kealahorn
John Jenkins
Samuel Allen
John Gray
Samuel Dickson
Miles Cauly

Patrick Roach
Jeremiah Murphy
George Fitzgaral
William Hurley
Mary Butler
Eloner Nowlan
David Stockman
Andrew Chabrito
Bryan Marran
James Meaglan and wife
Thomas Duane
John Thumb
Samuel Henry
Robert Heanary
Grace Gore
Pres. Pullen
John Mealon
Jany Quales
Jacob Magar

Robert Magan
Robert Main
Andrew Beard
William More
James Wiley, wife and
    two sisters
Thomas Miller, wife and
    son
Mary Wiley
Betty Wiley
Jane Wiley
John Fairservice
John Miller
Betty Ramaige
Jane Shanan
Jane Patterson
Michael Keanan

The passenger list of the brig *Willmott* from Cork, Ireland, which arrived on November 15, was comprised of:

Matthias Brett
Luke Welch
Mary Cockery
Catharine Sullivan
Catharine Connor
Margaret Ross
John Gibson
Joseph Mosses
Ann Dougale
Robert Dougale
William How
Jeremiah Davis
Thomas Dougale
Jonas Dougale
Abigail Dudley
Timothy Bryan
Austin McCarty
David Quirk
William Donshir
Ann Dougle
William Quirk
James Coghlin
John Murphy
Dennis Mahony

Margaret Mahony
John Hayes
John Henderson
James Ross
John Ross
John Ross, Jr.
Jane Ross
Darby Lawler
Catherine Carrill
Daniel Keefe
Matthew Howard
Thomas Quinlan
John King
Charles Hewett
James Dalton
Cornelius Fox
Peter McNamara
Daniel Carthy
Patrick Welch
John Kelly
Barbara Kelly
Peter Manning
Arthur Veavea
Redmond Larnard

Cornelius Hagarty
Edmond Swaney
Daniel Buckley
Cornelius Sullivan
Bat. Sullivan
George Shinnehan
William Kahaven
William Fitzgerald
Edward Murphy
John Twahy
Catherine Twahy
William Stephens
James Row
Isabella Learman
John Bourke
Patrick Ryan
John Bowler
Mary Dougle
John Dowle
James O'Daniel
Thomas McCarty
John Lee

Other arrivals, 1766:

Henry Higgins
Edward Carey
Edward Griffin
John Mahan
Richard Quirk
Thomas Roach
Luke McGray
Thomas Barrey
William Comings
Thomas Whaland
Samuel White
William Finley
Ann Callehan and two children
Norris Dayley

James Casey
John Murrey
James Cochran
John Barry
Mrs. Dunn
Margaret Driskel
Matthew McNamara
Robert Morisey
James Burn
Thomas Kenady
Darby Rion
John Hanbury
Nathaniel Linch
Luke Dulin
Morris Murphy

Philip Dunelty
Pattrick Brinnen
Edward Whalin
John Hade
John McDonough
John Fling
John Gleason
Thomas Fling
James Lase
Jesse Connelly
Thomas Power
William Murphy
Elizabeth Cotter
Michael Carrell

1767.

Mary Roche
———— McConnel
Elizabeth Corbet
Daniel McBrine
William Fitchgeral
Elizabeth McKew
John Duffy
Patrick Caroline
Owen Caroline
Lawrence Merren

Carrick McRoss
James Fitchpatrick
Timothy Ward
William Lawren
Henry Gibbons
Patrick McMasters
Daniel Morrison
Michael Grant
Charles Hart
William Kirby

Timothy Flaharty
Dan. McHaney
Jeremiah Kane
William McKeen
Edward McDaniel
John Savage
Richard Malony
Thomas McDonogh
Michael Darcy
James Kelly

The full complement of passengers on the brig *Ann and Margaret*, which arrived from Ireland on October 14, 1767, was:

Eleanor Murphy
Eleanor McSweney
Francis Hodrett
Mary Machoon
Mary Howard
John Kinney
Elizabeth Brien
Ann Collins
Judith Pop
Edward Dammarell
Mary Callahane
Mary Conun
Eleanor Moloney
Timothy Mulcahy
George Prickard
Samuel Prickard

Thomas Prickard
Paul Prickard
Dinish McSweney
James Conner
Darby Conner
Mary Wilkinson
Eleanor Stokes
Mary Ambrose
Mary O'Brien
John Jackson
John Lyndsay
John Murphy
Margaret Fleming
Elizabeth Wilkenson
Honer Coveney
Edward France

Ann Hill
Mary Stoaks
William Sweney
James Fitzgerrald
William Hoban
John Baker
John Furch
Isaac Stoakes
Richard Terutch
Joseph King
Edmond Shanohan
M. Byrn
Dinish Rien
William Buck
Philip O'Donel

1768.

Patrick Conner
—— Glynn
John Kilbany
John Mallone
John Finley
Patrick Dupee
Patrick Ham
Mrs. McKennedy
William McCartey
Mr. Larey
William Lawler
Daniel McClester
John Neace
Peter Griffen
Edward Griffen
Sallie McCartie

Felix McMean
Juda McMean
Mary O'Bryan
Patrick Toben
John Terrey
John Tracy
Nicholas Whealan
Michael Conner
Michael Coleman
Daniel Connel
Edmund Maugher
Thomas Coady
Michael Collins
Patrick Hannan
William Buckley
Walter Flanen

James Magee
Edward McCarty
Edward Welch
Edward Linch
James Hickey
Terence McCarty
John Burke
Dan Hogan
John Madock
John Dunfee
James Mahane
James Rowland
John Dehany
John Dalton
John Murphy

1769.

Mrs. Swiney
Mrs. Henesey

John Gallikan
Joseph Carell

Hannah Dwier
Patrick Briant

EARLY RECORDS OF PORTSMOUTH, N. H.

MARRIAGES—EXTRACTED FROM RECORDS KEPT BY JOSHUA PEIRCE, TOWN CLERK AND PROVINCIAL RECORDER OF DEEDS, NOW IN POSSESSION OF THE NEW ENGLAND HISTORICAL AND GENEALOGICAL SOCIETY.

COPIED BY MICHAEL J. O'BRIEN.

"John Parkes of Dublin in Ireland and Susanna Preston w^r marry^d 14 Oct. 1716."

"James Berry of Dublin in Ireland and Mehittable Leach w^r marry^d 18 Oct. 1716."

"James Wals (Walsh?) of Dublin in Ireland in Great Brittain and Mary Sanders of Portsm^o w^r marry^d ye 16 Jany. 1717–8."

"Jno Kincade of Waterford in Ireland in Great Brittain and Martha Churchill of Portsm^o w^r marry^d 13 No. 1718."

"Saml Hewey of Coldrain in ye County of Derry in Ireland in Great Brittain and Elizabeth Denett wid^o of Portsm^o w^r marry^d 23 Dec. 1718."

22

"David Horrey of Gallway in Ireland and Eliz^th Broughton of Portsm° w^r marry^d No^r 1720."

"Jn° Henderson of Coldraine in ye county of Derrye in Ireland and Sarah Keel of Portsm° were marry^d 1 Jany. 1721–2."

"Jn° Larye of Ireland in ye County of Cork and Hannah Tout of Portsm° w^r marry^d 16 June 1723."

"Patrick Lawley of——and Eliz^th Churchill of Portsm° w^r marry^d 18th Sept. 1724."

"Jam^s ffadden of Coldkain in ye County of Antrim in Ireland and Hannah Shute of Portsm° were marry^d 8 Ap. 1726."

"Jam^s Kenny of Cadteen in ye county of Terrone in Ireland in Great Britain and Lydia Linsby wid° of Portsm° w^r marry^d 17 Nov. 1726."

"George Taylor of Saint Mary's Parish in Limerick in ye kingdom of Ireland and Sarah Phicket of Postm° w^r marry^d 23^d of June 1736."

"Samuel Miller born in ye County of Derry in Ireland and Margaret Calwell w^r marry^d ye 25th of Novr. 1736."

"James Wason of ye Parish of Bellemanus in ye County of Antrim in Ireland and Hannah Calwell of ye same place w^r marry^d ye 30th of Novr. 1736."

"Daniel Grant and Catharine McBride w^r marry^d the 14th of March 1736."

"John Larey of Portsm° and Rachel White of Stratham w^r marry^d 19th Decr. 1736."

"Willm Fling of ye Parish of Killrick in the County of Waterford and Jean Cook of ye county of Tipperary both in Ireland w^r marry^d ye 18th of Decr 1737."

"Adam Templeton of ye County of Antrim and Parish of Bellawille and Margret Lendsey of ye County of Derry both in ye Kingdom of Ireland was marry^d 12th of April 1739."

"Robert Beard of Nottingham Born in Colerain in ye Kingdom of Ireland and Grissoll Beverland of the same Kingdom w^r marry^d 27th of Novr. 1739."

"Mathew Nealy of Nottingham Born at Billycarry in ye County of Derry in ye Kingdom of Ireland and Margret Beverland of ye same kingdom were marry^d ye 27th of Nov. 1739."

"Joseph Connor and Mary Sevey were marry^d ye 25th of Jan. 1738."

"Alex^r Callwel of ye County of Antrim in ye Parish of Clough in Ireland and Margret Macgregore of Londonderry in N-Hamp^r w^r marry^d Nov. 4th 1741."

"Isaac Miller and Mary Tomson of County of Derry In the Parish of Dunbo in ye kingdom of Ireland now of Portsm° w^r marry^d March 9th 1741-2."

"Mark Cook born at York in Va. and Sarah Maddin born in Limerick in ye King^m of Ireland w^r marry^d Decr. 22^d 1740."

"Daniel Kelly and Joan Riyan both of Limerick in ye Kingdom of Ireland w^r marry^d Jany. 15th 1740-1."

"Daniel McCleres Born àt Affeody in county of Derry in Ireland and Elizabeth Tomson Born at Bellewoolin in ye County of Antrim in ye same Kingdom w^r marry^d 8th of Apr^l. 1740."

FROM THE TOWN RECORDS OF PORTSMOUTH.

"1686, July 20th—The Selectmen gave a warrant to the Constable to warn John Kelley, Peter Harvie, John Ried^and 'Mis' Stocker before the Selectmen to give an account of their being in towne and for Harvie's entertaining strangers without liberty."

"1686, July 24th—John Kelley being examined for bringing his Wife and 2 children into towne without leave was warned by the Selectmen to give security from saving the town from any charge of himself and wife and children or to depart. He then promised he would within a week. Peter Harvie being questioned for entertaining his sister and 2 children said he would get security speedily."

SOME PORTSMOUTH TAXPAYERS IN 1727.

John Fitzgerald.	Peter Greeley.
James Dun.	James Mackeny.
David Horney.	Stephen Pendergrass.
Jeremiah Lawry.	Daniel Quirk.

Patrick Garey.

RESIDENTS OF PORTSMOUTH WHO SIGNED THE REVOLUTIONARY
PLEDGE IN 1776.

Robert Furniss.	Matthew Haslett.	James Ryan.
Richard Fitzgerald.	James Haslett.	David Maclure.
Edward Dempsey.	Robert Neall.	Hugh McBride.
Jeremiah Clancy.	James Dwyer.	A. McIntyre.
Edmond Butler.	James Driscol.	James McInter.
Thomas Hayley.	John Collins.	John Mackmahawn.

GENERAL PIERSE LONG OF PORTSMOUTH, N. H.

Pierse Long, the father of Brigadier-General Pierse Long of
Revolutionary fame, was born in Limerick, Ireland, about the
beginning of the eighteenth century and served an apprentice-
ship with a merchant of that city, who exported goods to the
colonies. By him he was sent to Portsmouth in the year 1730,
where he opened a store and continued to receive consignments
of goods from Ireland. He purchased cargoes of lumber and
other articles for shipment to the West Indies market, and, before
his death in 1740, was reputed to be one of the wealthiest merchants of the Province.

Pierse Long, Jr., was born at Portsmouth in 1739. He was
an active patriot of the Revolution and, when the war broke out,
he was chosen one of the delegates to the first Provincial Congress at Exeter. He was on the Committee of Safety and was
with Sullivan and Langdon at the surprise of the fort in Portsmouth harbor in 1774, when the English guns and ammunition.
which were used with telling effect six months later at Bunker
Hill, were captured. He filled various offices under the province
and town until May, 1776, when he was appointed to the command of the First New Hampshire Regiment, with Hercules
Mooney as lieutenant-colonel. The regiment continued to be
stationed at the forts around Portsmouth harbor until October,
1776, when it received orders to march to the Canadian border,
near Lake Champlain. There he reported to General St. Clair
and was assigned to the command of Fort Independence on the
lake, with his own and Colonel Carlton's regiments, and at the
same time was appointed brigadier-general.

In June, 1777, when General St. Clair determined to abandon his position on Lake Champlain, on account of the advance of General Burgoyne with 10,000 English, Canadians, Tories and Indians, he entrusted to Long the command of the flotilla which was to transfer the entire American force of 3,000 men to Lake George. On July 6, while proceeding to Saratoga, he was overtaken at Fort Ann by a British regiment; an action ensued, in which the British were beaten and forced to retreat. About this time, the period for which the troops had enlisted having expired, they asked for and received their discharge—all except the colonel and four men, one of whom was his faithful personal servant, James Mullen. These, with the colonel, proceeded to Saratoga and there volunteered their services to the commander-in-chief and assisted at the capture of Burgoyne.

Colonel Long, being attacked with a serious illness, was obliged to retire. When he recovered, he returned to Portsmouth and resumed his mercantile business, which had been sadly neglected. Between 1784 and 1786, he was a delegate to Congress and from 1786 to 1789 he was state senator. When Washington was chosen president, he appointed Colonel Long, Collector of the Customs at Portsmouth, but, before he could take office, he died, on April 3, 1789. He is described as "a handsome, portly man, of unblemished Christian character, amiable and courteous, a correct merchant and a good soldier." His daughters were remarkable for their great personal beauty. One of them, Mary, married Colonel Tobias Lear, private secretary to George Washington. His son, George Long, became a very wealthy merchant and ship owner.

SOME INTERESTING SHIPPING STATISTICS OF THE EIGHTEENTH CENTURY.

BY MICHAEL J. O'BRIEN.

Although it is admitted by many competent authorities that natives of Ireland settled in the American Colonies in great numbers during the seventeenth and eighteenth centuries, there is now no means of determining the precise number of people who came in these continuous emigrations. No official statistics were kept in Colonial days, and it was not until the year 1819 that Congress provided for a record of arrivals from foreign countries. There are, however, many sources from which reliable—and, indeed, undeniable—estimates may be formed of the comparative extent of Irish immigration; such, for example, as the Land Records and Council Journals of the original Thirteen Colonies, the Court Records, the Church Registers, the Town Books, the rosters of the troops organized during the Indian, French and Revolutionary wars and other similarly authentic sources.

A few years ago, I published some extracts taken from the records of the Land Offices and Church Records of Maryland, North Carolina and other Southern States. I gave the names of a very large number of Irish people who received grants of land in that section, and of Irish names which appear in the Will Books, the Birth, Marriage and Death Registers of the Churches and so on. I showed, by the dates and the names and by the relation of many incidents and events with which these people were connected, that the human tide began to flow hitherward from Ireland as early as the year 1650 and continued, in more or less strength, down to the period of the Revolution and in almost perfect consonance with the changes and vicissitudes in Irish fortunes. I distributed some of this material among historical societies and received many letters expressing surprise that, while the records appear so readily accessible to our people, we have not availed ourselves of them, but instead, have continued to complain of unfair treatment at the hands of those who have no interest whatever in anything Irish and should not be expected to have. My correspondents are absolutely right. We ought to quit complaining and do for our own what others have done for theirs, and if we had done so long before now, I believe we would hear very little to-day of "the Scotch-Irish and the Anglo-Saxon, who, to the exclusion of all others, laid the foundations of the American Republic."

Among the many sources from which data on this subject may be obtained are the newspapers of the period. In pursuing my researches for a forthcoming work on the contributions of Irish schoolmasters to the education of Colonial youth, I have made an examination of a number of New York and Philadelphia newspapers of the eighteenth century, from which I have extracted some very interesting facts. Among these are many notices of ships sailing to and from American and Irish ports, advertisements by Irish merchants'and of Irish-manufactured goods for sale by the shopkeepers of the day, advertisements by the postmasters of letters addressed to recent Irish arrivals, and numerous other announcements of a miscellaneous character in which Irish people "figured" to a large extent.

While the passenger lists of the ships are not given in any case, I think it can hardly be denied that the fact that so many vessels were plying between American and Irish ports in those days, and while the French-English war was on, is an indication that there must have been a constant stream of emigration flowing from Ireland to America during the eighteenth century. All of the ships mentioned were passenger-carrying vessels. In fact, the owners' advertisements in the newspapers usually announced that they had ample, and in some instances "extraordinary," accommodation for passengers, and I find, in many cases where sailings for Ireland only were announced, the home ports of those vessels were in that country. For the purpose of the present paper, I have selected the announcements in one newspaper only, viz: *The New York Gazette and Weekly Post-Boy* of the years 1750 to 1758. Among the "Ships registered at the New York Custom House, " with names of captains, dates of sailing, clearance or arrival, I find the following:

SAILINGS FROM THE PORT OF NEW YORK.

Date.		Name of Vessel.	Name of Master.	Destination
1750				
Jan	8	Snow *Unicorn*	James Ackland	Dublin
Jan	22	Snow *Ross*	George Duncan	Belfast
Jan.	29	Snow *Needham*	Duncan Brown	Newry in Ireland
April	23	Sloop *Virgin*	Joseph Smith	Ireland
June	18	Snow *Swift*	J. Dyatt	Ireland
Nov.	5	Brig *Warren*	J. McCracken	Belfast
Nov.	2	Snow *Britania*	B. Winthrop	Londonderry
Nov.	12	Brig *John and Mary*	Adam Fisher	Newry in Ireland
Nov.	12	Ship *Grace*	John Nealson	Belfast
Nov.	26	Ship *Dover*	William Richards	Belfast and Newry
Dec.	10	Snow *Jacob*	Jos. Carpenter	Newry
1751				
Jan.	7	Snow *New York*	John Gifford	Newry in Ireland
Jan.	7	Snow *Betsy and Rachel*	Jos. Riddel	Dublin
Jan.	28	Brig *Funchal*	J. Harrison	Londonderry
Oct.	21	Snow *Needham*	W. Collins	Newry in Ireland
Oct.	28	Brig *Catherine*	James Devereaux	Ireland
Nov.	14	Snow *Charming Sally*	Thomas White	Londonderry

Date.	Name of Vessel.	Name of Master.	Destination.
1751			
Nov. 14	Snow *Antrim*	W. Woodlock	Belfast
Nov. 25	Snow *Entwistle*	John Smith	Belfast
Dec. 2	Snow *Marsden*	Michael Jordan	Dublin
Dec. 2	Snow *New York*	J. Gifford	Dublin
Dec. 9	Brig ———	Joseph Devereaux	Cork
Dec. 9	Brig *Gregg*	John Allen	Belfast
Dec. 9	Ship *Four Cantons*	C. Heysham	Dublin & Swanzey
Dec. 9	Snow *Success*	Francis Boggs	Londonderry
1752			
Jan. 20	Brig *Warren*	J. McCracken	Belfast in Ireland
Jan. 27	Snow *Sally*	Neil McNeill	Newry in Ireland
Feb. 20	Brig *Prince*	Luke Troy	Belfast in Ireland
April 27	Brig *Spadil*	Alexr. Hope	Ireland
June 8	Snow *Rose and Peggy*	Hans Thode	Dublin
Nov. 20	Snow *Charming Sally*	Thomas White	Dublin
Nov. 20	Brig *Gordon*	Anthony McMillan	Belfast
Nov. 20	Snow *Success*	Francis Boggs	Londonderry
Nov. 27	Brig *Nelly*	James McElveny	Coleraine
Dec. 11	Snow *Friendship*	Thomas Marshal	Londonderry
Dec. 11	Snow *William*	John McLean	Belfast
Dec. 11	Brig *Prince*	Luke Troy	Sligo in Ireland
Dec. 18	Brig St. *Paul*	John Finley	Newry in Ireland
Dec. 25	Ship *Prince George*	James Falls	Londonderry
Dec. 25	Snow *Antrim*	W. Woodlock	Belfast
1753			
Jan. 15	Sloop *Melling*	Hugh McQuaid	Newry in Ireland
Feb. 5	Brig St. *Andrew*	Robert Donaldson	Newry
Feb. 5	Brig *Polly*	Bernard Badger	Londonderry
Feb. 5	Snow *Ross*	George Duncan	Belfast in Ireland
Feb. 19	Sloop *Kitty*	Theophilus Barnes	Newry in Ireland
Feb. 19	Ship *Beulah*	John Richey	Newry in Ireland
Feb. 26	Sloop *Fanny*	Patrick Nealson	Dublin
June 14	Snow *Hauk*	John Brown	Belfast & Cork
April 14	Brig *Prince*	Luke Troy	Londonderry
July 16	Sloop *Messalina*	Alexr. Sloan	Cork in Ireland
Nov. 19	*Prince William*	Lawrence Bishop	Londonderry
Nov. 19	Snow *Henry*	Charles Stewart	Belfast in Ireland
Dec. 24	Ship *Grace*	Edward McAllister	Belfast in Ireland
Dec. 24	Ship *Charming Rachel*	John McCleave	Dublin
1754			
July 8	Snow *Unicorn*	John Wallace	Cork in Ireland
Dec. 16	Brig *Nelly*	James McElveney	Coleraine
Dec. 16	Snow *Prince Wales*	Patrick Nealson	Newry
1755			
Jan. 6	Brig *Egmont*	James Rea	Cork
Jan. 6	Snow *Edinburgh*	John French	Newry
Jan. 13	Ship *Adventure*	Joseph Jackson	Newry & Dublin
Jan. 13	Ship *Annabella*	John Woodhouse	Newry
June 2	Snow *Magog*	Isaac Sheldon	Cork in Ireland
Dec. 8	Snow *Belvidere*	James Lamport	Drogheda in Ireland
1756			
Feb. 6	Ship *Molly*	David Gregory	Dublin
Feb. 6	Snow *Friendship*	Patrick Boyle	Newry
June 14	Snow *Four Cantons*	C. Heysham	Dublin
Dec. 27	*Duke of Argyle*	William King	Newry & Glasgow

Date.		Name of Vessel.	Name of Master.	Destination.
1756				
Dec.	27	Ship *Seahorse*	Francis Blair	Newry
Dec.	27	Ship *Union*	John Cowan	Dublin & Liverpool
Dec.	5	Brig *Achilles*	Robert Brown	Cork
Dec.	12	Ship *Hibernia*	?	Newry
1757				
Dec.	19	Brig *Molly*	Richard Nevill	Sligo in Ireland
1758				
Jan.	16	Ship *Lucy*	Robert Willson	Drogheda
Jan.	23	Brig *Achilles*	Robert Brown	Cork & Newry
Feb.	6	Snow *Drednought*	James McLaughlin	Londonderry
Feb.	6	Ship *Blakeney*	William Moore	Londonderry
Feb.	6	Snow *Lord Dunluce*	John Mansod	Larne & Belfast
Feb.	13	Snow *William*	Robert McLeith	Newry
Feb.	13	Snow *Neil Gilles*	?	Newry & Glasgow
Feb.	20	Snow *Sally*	Francis Moore	Dublin & Liverpool
Feb.	27	Snow *Jenny*	William Willcock	Dublin
Feb.	27	Ship *Moore*	Richard Moore	Newry
March	6	Snow *Four Cantons*	C. Heysham	Dublin
March	6	Ship *Hopewell*	Francis Falls	Londonderry
March	13	Brig *Edward*	John Brown	Newry
May	29	Brig *Seaflower*	John Williams	Cork
Oct.	10	Snow *Lord Howe*	William Moore	Dublin
Oct.	9	Ship *Earl of Dunnegall*	J. McBride	Ireland
Dec.	4	Ship *Susannah*	Thomas Dunbar	Newry and Dublin
Dec.	4	Snow *General Wolfe*	William Moore	Dublin
Dec.	4	Ship *Dublin*	Boyl Moss	Dublin

ARRIVALS AT THE PORT OF NEW YORK.

Date.		Name of Vessel.	Name of Master.	Where from.
1750				
Nov.	12	Galley *Bendal*	Davis Bendal	Londonderry
Nov.	26	Snow *Antrim*	W. Woodlock	Liverpool & Ireland
1751				
June	24	Snow *Britannia*	B. Winthrop	Dublin & Bristol
Dec.	2	Brig *Warren*	J. McCracken	Belfast
April	27	Snow *William*	James Richards	Bristol & Cork
Nov.	13	Snow *Antrim*	Wm. Woodlock	Carrickfergus
Dec.	11	Snow *Ross*	George Duncan	Belfast & Liverpool
1752				
April	16	Sloop *Sally*	Captain White	Dublin
July	2	Snow *Charming Sally*	Thomas White	Dublin
July	2	Brig *Prince*	Luke Troy	Cork in Ireland
Aug.	13	Sloop *Fanny*	Patrick Nealson	Liverpool & Cork
Aug.	13	Ship *Charming* ——	Thomas White	Waterford in Ireland
Nov.	19	Ship *Drednought*	James McLoughlin	Dublin
Nov.	19	Snow *Antrim*	Robert McCalmont	Port Carrickfergus
Nov.	26	Snow *Leigh*	Thomas Hodgson	Dublin & Liverpool
1755				
Dec.	8	Snow *Boyne*	Patrick Martin	Drogheda
Dec.	8	Snow *Antrim*	James Wallace	Carrickfergus
1756				
June	28	Ship *Earl of Holderness*	William Simpson	Cork
July	25	Sloop *Charming Molly*	J. Grigg	Dublin & Cork

Date.		Name of Vessel.	Name of Master.	Where from.
1757				
Nov.	9	Snow *Boyne*	Patrick Martin	Drogheda
Nov.	21	Brig *Mary*	John Keiting	Waterford in Irelaɪ
Nov.	28	Ship *Delahanty*	Joseph Blair	Dublin
Dec.	20	Brig *Nelly*	James McElveny	Coleraine
Dec.	27	Snow *Sally*	Francis Moore	Dublin
1758				
Feb.	6	Snow *Four Cantons*	C. Heysham	Dublin
Feb.	6	Snow *Lord Russell*	James Hathorne	Belfast
March	6	Snow *Charming Sally*	H. Dunscomb	Londonderry
Oct.	23	Sloop *Drednought*	Captain Dougherty	Londonderry
Nov.	20	Ship *Willey*	John McConnell	Londonderry
Nov.	20	Snow *Four Cantons*	John Tasker	Dublin
Nov.	27	Snow *Lord Dunluce*	John Munsed	Larne
Dec.	4	Ship *Culloden*	John Carr	Londonderry
Dec.	11	Snow *Morning Star*	Michael Walsh	Cork

Ships Commanded by Irish-Named Captains, Sailing to and from the Port of New York.

1750, April   2—Sloop *Peggy*, Robert Keily, for Antigua.

April   9—Snow *Elizabeth*, James McHugh, for St. Kitts.

July   23—Brig *John and Mary*, Dennis Roche, for Honduras.

July   23—Snow *Dumb Eagle*, J. Connell, for Lisbon.

Nov.   5—Sloop *Farmer's Tryal*, Daniel Higgins, from North Carolina.

1751, March   2—Schooner *Catharine*, Michael McNemara, for Boston.

April   15—Ship *Antilope*, John Ryan, from Honduras.

Sept.   2—Schooner *Shannon*, Pat. Holeran for Antigua.

Oct.   4—Sloop *Tryal*, Patrick Harrold, for Tortola.

Dec.   9—Sloop *Peggy*, L. Flanagan, for Jamaica.

1752, Oct.   30—Sloop *Polly*, Patrick Mitchel, for Jamaica.

1753, July   16—Schooner *Arnold*, Patrick Boyle, to New Jersey and Ship *John*, Richard Coffey, for Canary Islands.

1753, July   23—Sloop *Polly*, Patrick Mitchel, to South Carolina.

1753, July   30—Ship *Marlboro*, William Barry, for London.

1753, Oct.   1—Sloop *Hannah and Mary*, David Higgins for Virginia.

1754,   —Snow *Ruddock*, John Doyle, for Barbadoes.

1754, Nov.   25—Sloop *Priscilla*, Patrick Boyle (destination not stated).

1755, Jan.   13—Sloop *Morning Star*, Michael Keating, to Virginia and Sloop *Success*, John Buckley to Bermuda.

Sept.   22—Sloop *Lake George*, Anthony McMullen, to North Carolina.

1756, Oct.   18—Sloop *Charming Sally*, William O'Brien, from Philadelphia.

Dec.   13—Sloop *Charming Polly*, William O'Brien, for Providence.

Dec.   20—Schooner *Seaflower*, Henry O'Brian, from Halifax.

1757, Sept.   20—Schooner *Warner*, Daniel Sullivan, from Antigua.

1758, Feb.   13—Ship *George*, Michael Dalton, for Jamaica.

March   13—Schooner *Charming Polly*, Matthew McNamara, for Halifax.

July   3—Ship *King of Prussia*, Walter McAuley, for Jamaica.

Aug.   21—Ship *Greyhound*, Lawrence Farrell, for Halifax.

Oct.   2—Ship *Greyhound*, Richard Power, for Philadelphia.

Oct.   30—Schooner *King Fisher*, John Ryan, from Boston.

DESPATCHES FROM PHILADELPHIA PUBLISHED IN THE NEW YORK GAZETTE AND WEEKLY POST-BOY, UNDER THE CAPTION "REGISTERED AT THE CUSTOM HOUSE."

(Years 1750 to 1752 only copied. Names of the vessels are not given.)

SAILINGS FROM PHILADELPHIA.

Date.	Names of Captains.	Destination.
1750		
March 5	Rees	Dublin
March 5	McClelland	Newry
April 5	Keefe	Dublin
May 14	Ash	Dublin
June 25	Henderson	Cork
July 9	Plawson	Cork
July 16	Wheelwright	Dublin
Aug. 20	Ambler	Cork
Aug. 27	Dunbar	Dublin
Sept. 3	Morrison	Cork
Sept. 10	Cameron	Dublin
Sept. 17	Caldwell	Cork
Oct. 1	Carr	Cork
Oct. 8	Mason	Cork
Oct. 8	Forrest	Cork
Oct. 10	Bogs	Cork
Oct. 15	Johnson	Ireland
Oct. 22	Stewart	Newry
Oct. 29	Bowne	Cork
Oct. 29	Erwin	Coleraine
Nov. 5	Brown	Londonderry
Nov. 12	Mitchell	Londonderry
Nov. 12	Fall	Londonderry
Nov. 12	Dunbar	Belfast
Nov. 19	Dunn	Dublin
Nov. 26	Edwards	Newry
Nov. 26	Mason	Cork
Nov. 26	Erwin	Cork
Nov. 26	Moore	Londonderry
Dec. 3	Blair	Belfast
Dec 17	Cameron	Londonderry
Dec. 17	Edwards	Newry
Dec. 17	Woodside	Londonderry
Dec. 31	Hamilton	Dublin

Date.	Names of Captains.	Destination.
1751		
March 11	Troy	Dublin
April 22	Snead	Cork & Dublin
May 27	Blair	Dublin
June 6	Slade	Dublin
June 3	Cuthbert	Dublin
July 8	Brown	Cork
Aug. 5	Leech	Cork
Aug. 19	Stewart	Cork
Sept. 9	Mitchell	Cork
Sept. 16	McGee	Dublin
Sept. 16	Stuart	Cork
Sept. 16	Fitzgerald	Cork
Sept. 23	Leaths	Waterford
Oct. 17	Moore	Londonderry
Oct. 17	Henderson	Cork
Oct. 17	Hawkins	Cork
Oct. 17	Macilvaine	Cork
Oct. 14	Spurrier	Cork
Nov. 4	Kerr	Londonderry
Nov. 4	McCormick	Belfast
Nov. 18	Dunwell	Cork
Nov. 18	Peele	Cork
Nov. 18	Moore	Londonderry
Nov. 25	Farrar	Ireland
Nov. 25	Davis	Cork
Nov. 25	Brown	Cork
Nov. 25	Mitchell	Londonderry
Dec. 2	Woodside	Newry
Dec. 2	Cameron	Newry
Dec. 2	Dun	Newry
Dec. 2	Wallace	Newry
Dec. 16	Bishop	Ireland
Dec. 16	Wallace	Dublin
Dec. 16	Wright	Dublin
Dec. 16	Rea	Cork
Dec. 16	Montpelier	Cork
Dec. 16	Stewart	Newry
Dec. 30	Young	Newry
Dec. 30	Gill	Londonderry
Dec. 30	Bachop	Londonderry
1752		
March 2	Simpson	Dublin
March 2	Smith	Dublin
March 16	Dunn	Dublin

Date.	Names of Captains.	Destination.
1752		
March 16	Allison	Dublin
March 16	Stout	Cork
March 30	Harper	Dublin
April 6	Marshall	Cork
May 11	Morris	Dublin
May 11	Beesely	Cork
May 18	Arthur	Dublin
May 18	Appowen	Dublin
May 18	Flinn	Dublin
May 25	Brown	Cork
June 8	Giddings	Dublin
June 8	Arthur	Dublin
June 8	Brown	Dublin
June 15	Hayes	Cork
June 15	Farr	Cork
June 22	Snead	Dublin
June 22	Norarth	Cork
June 29	Brown	Cork
June 29	Nicholson	Dublin
June 29	Peel	Cork
July 6	Stokes	Dublin
July 6	Magee	Dublin
July 20	Taylor	Cork
July 27	Caldwell	Cork
Aug. 10	Stokes	Dublin
Aug. 31	Troy	Dublin
Aug. 31	Leethes	Waterford
Aug. 25	Heysham	Dublin
Oct. 9	Hope	Cork
Oct. 9	Moore	Cork
Oct. 30	Dresson	Newry
Nov. 13	Ross	Cork
Nov. 13	Simpson	Newry
Nov. 20	Collins	Waterford
Nov. 20	Stewart	Dublin
Nov. 27	Blair	Dublin
Nov. 27	McNamara	Coleraine
Dec. 4	Scott	Londonderry
Dec. 11	McGee	Newry
Dec. 11	Stewart	Newry
Dec. 11	Harrison	Dublin
Dec. 11	Harper	Cork
Dec. 11	Henderson	Londonderry
Dec. 25	Hatton	Londonderry
Dec. 25	Dunn	Londonderry

Date.		Names of Captains.	Destination.
1752			
Dec.	25	McIlvaine	Londonderry
Dec.	25	Stamper	Newry
Dec.	25	Simpson	Newry
Dec.	25	Cameron	Newry
Dec.	25	Peele	Belfast
Dec.	25	Herlowson	Dublin
Dec.	25	Blair	Dublin

ARRIVALS AT THE PORT OF PHILADELPHIA.

Date.		Names of Captains.	Where From.
1750			
April	16	Woodside	Liverpool & Coleraine
July	2	Martin	Belfast
Aug.	20	Duncan	Liverpool & Belfast
1751			
July	8	Dunbar	Dublin
Aug.	5	Leiths	Waterford
Sept.	23	Smith	Belfast
Sept.	23	Kerr	Ireland
Sept.	23	Breading	Lough Swilly
Sept.	23	Marshall	Londonderry
Nov.	11	Brown	Cork
Dec.	16	Smith	Dublin
Dec.	16	Blair	Ireland
1752			
March	2	Gass	Dublin
April	27	Appowen	Dublin
May	4	Beesley	Cork
May	25	Brown	Belfast
June	1	Davis	Cork
June	8	Noarth	Cork
June	15	Stokes	Dublin
June	15	Magee	Dublin
June	29	Brown	Cork
July	13	Wallace	Newry
July	27	Shelley	Waterford
Aug.	17	Hamilton	Belfast
Aug.	24	Harper	Dublin
Aug.	31	Stout	Dublin
Aug.	31	Mitchel	Londonderry
Oct.	2	Brown	Cork
Oct.	2	Appowin	Dublin
Oct.	2	Morris	Dublin
Oct.	16	Katter	Dublin
Nov.	20	MacIlvaine	Londonderry
Nov.	27	Stewart	Newry

NAMES TAKEN FROM NOTICES IN THE NEW YORK GAZETTE AND
WEEKLY POST-BOY, OF MASTERS OF VESSELS PLYING TO
AND FROM THE PORT OF PHILADELPHIA IN 1750 AND 1752.

Connors	Gallagher	Fitzsimmons
Caffary	Fitzgerald	Coffey
Kelly	Sheehan	Moriarty
Maloney	Connor	Hayes
Malley	Higgins	Killeran
Cahill	Dermot	Moore
Donnelly	Dunn	Rooney
McCarty	Ryan	Shiel
Magee	Mulloney	McKeen
McCormick	Shields	Barrett
Shannon	Driscall	
	Power	
	Kennedy	

RECORDS OF BURIALS AT CHRIST CHURCH, PHILADELPHIA.

COMMUNICATED BY MICHAEL J. O'BRIEN

Name.	Date.	Name.	Date.
John Bryan	July 26, 1734	Mary Cane	Jan. 2, 1739
Edward Buckley	May 27, 1718	Anne Cane	Jan. 26, 1750
Elizabeth Buckley	Feb. 20, 1733	James Cane	July 10, 1751
John Burck	Aug. 2, 1741	Walter Carley	June 18, 1732
John Burk	Jan. 4, 1742	John Carney	June 21, 1712
Elinor, wife of		William Cochrane	Mar. 17, 1736
Patrick Burk	May 3, 1748	Elizabeth, daughter of	
Joseph Burke	June 14, 1736	Cornelius Coffey	Sept. 8, 1734
Sarah Ann Burke	Jan. 13, 1737	Elinor Collins	Aug. 18, 1746
William Burke	Feb. 11, 1737	James Collins	Apr. 4, 1748
Margaret Burke	July 3, 1738	Isabel Collins	Nov. 19, 1733
Susannah Burke	Nov. 13, 1751	John Collins	Jan. 11, 1730
Elizabeth, wife of		Elizabeth Collins	Sept. 19, 1736
Thomas Burn	Aug. 17, 1735	Thomas Collins	Oct. 4, 1737
John Callahan	Feb. 12, 1749	William Collins	May 22, 1739
Mary, daughter of		Anne Collins	Aug. 22, 1739
Morris Callahoon	Oct. 27, 1759	Mary Collins	Nov. 22, 1739
———, son of		James Collins	Mar. 15, 1743
Patrick Canaday,	Sept. 4, 1756	Catherine Collins	Nov. 20, 1744

Name.	Date.	Name.	Date.
Sarah Collins	Oct. 6, 1746	John Dugan	Apr. 21, 1731
William Collins	Sept. 13, 1747	William. Dun	Oct. 15, 1710
John Collins	Nov. 24, 1750	John Dun	Oct. 28, 1747
Edward Collins	June 20, 1752	Eloner Dunn	Dec. 18, 1743
Mary Collohan	June 20, 1758	Jeremiah Dunnahan	Aug. 9, 1751
William Connally	Dec. 23, 1736	Peter Dunnavan	Dec. 5, 1746
William, son of		Jane Dunnavan	July 22, 1747
Patrick Connely	May 8, 1748	John Dunnavan	July 22, 1747
Bryan Connoly	Apr. 18, 1756	John Durgan	Jan. 5, 1757
William Connoly	Sept. 30, 1758	John Durgan	Mar. 13, 1759
Michael Connor	Mar. 31, 1730	Susannah Ennis	Sept. 17, 1731
John Connor	May 24, 1752	Mary Fagan	Apr. 24, 1739
Michael Connor	May 16, 1758	Mary Fagan	Jan. 19, 1747
Margaret Conoway	Dec. 4, 1727	Henry Fagan	Nov. 4, 1756
Bradford Conrahy	May 14, 1741	Mary Ann Farrel	Dec. 12, 1736
Margaret Conry	Mar. 16, 1730	William Farrel	Nov. 12, 1750
Martha Conway	Feb. 5, 1723	John Feagan	Jan. 6, 1743
William Corbett	Nov. 28, 1715	Sylvester Fitzharris	May 6, 1737
Joseph Corbett	Oct. 18, 1716	John Fitzharris	Oct. 10, 1738
Margaret, wife of		John Fitzharris	Jan. 13, 1742
Michael Coyle	Sept. 29, 1740	Peter Fitz Harris	July 25, 1746
Peter Coyle	Sept. 7, 1747	John Fitz Harris	Aug. 2, 1752
Patrick Cranfield	May 31, 1748	Hugh Fitzpatrick	June 2, 1731
William Croley	Mar. 1, 1726	John Flanahan	June 6, 1741
Mary, wife of		Patrick Fleming	Apr. 5, 1712
Daniel Cummings	Dec. 22, 1738	Thomas Fleming	Mar. 11, 1726
Anne Cummings	Dec. 11, 1727	Benjamin Fleming	Aug. 15, 1733
Richard Cummings	Feb. 15, 1730	Thomas Flemming	Nov. 10, 1728
Sarah Cummings	Oct. 22, 1739	Robert Flemming	Feb. 15, 1751
Elizabeth Cummins	June 4, 1720	Mary, daughter of	
Edith Cummins	Nov. 2, 1722	Matthew Fling	Jan. 21, 1747
John Cummins	Dec. 14, 1740	George, son of	
Susannah Cusack	June 16, 1753	Owen Fling	June 6, 1751
William Cusick	Sept. 5, 1747	Marbe Fling	June 16, 1752
John Daily	Nov. 21, 1755	John Fling	Aug. 12, 1752
Margaret Dalton	Sept. 12, 1747	George Fling	Feb. 25, 1753
Mary Daly	Sept. 30, 1740	John Fling	Nov. 13, 1756
Daniel Deley	Oct. 26, 1749	Hannah Fling	Aug. 20, 1758
Elizabeth Donalon	Dec. 10, 1745	John Fling	Oct. 15, 1759
George Dougherty	Dec. 26, 1754	Robert Fling	Oct. 11, 1759
James Dougherty	June 27, 1759	Anthony, son of	
Elizabeth Downey	July 15, 1746	Patrick Flood	Mar. 26, 1745
Simon Downey	Dec. 6, 1756	Samuel Flood	Aug. 12, 1746
John Doyle	July 27, 1733	Elizabeth Garrett	June 20, 1740
Thomas Doyle	Feb. 17, 1742	Hester Garvey	July 24, 1746
John Doyle	Jan. 3, 1755	John Garvey	Sept. 6, 1746

Name.	Date.	Name.	Date.
Joseph Gaven	Jan. 19, 1743	Chas. McCarty	Feb. 4, 1733
Elizabeth Gavin	July 7, 1747	Sarah McCarty	Oct. 2, 1746
Ann Geary	Feb. 5, 1744	William McCall	Mar. 6, 1729
Mary Gibbons	July 2, 1754	Margaret McCall	Mar. 14, 1731
Robert Giggins	Aug. 27, 1759	William McCall	May 15, 1736
Mary Gill	July 20, 1752	William McCall	Feb. 15, 1739
Joseph Gill	Mar. 13, 1753	Jane McCall	Jan. 11, 1740
William Gill	Dec. 21, 1759	Samuel McCall	July 19, 1740
Nicholas Gillingham	Jan. 13, 1745	George McCall	Oct. 15, 1740
William Gillum	July 9, 1741	John McCall	Aug. 15, 1741
Patrick Grame	May 29, 1731	Jasper McCall	July 27, 1745
Anne Grogan	Oct. 1, 1757	Mary McCall	Aug. 15, 1745
James Grogan	Aug. 25, 1758	George McCall	Dec. 17, 1745
Samuel Higgins	Sept. 30, 1759	Anne McCall	Jan. 16, 1746
Thomas Hines	Mar. 24, 1743	Mary McCall	July 1, 1747
Peter Hynes	Apr. 18, 1756	Margaret McCarvill	Dec. 18, 1753
Thomas Hynds	Apr. 4, 1759	Elizabeth McClannan	Aug. 9, 1746
Margaret Joyce	Oct. 4, 1713	Anne, wife of Dennis	
William Kane	July 19, 1725	McClocklin	Mar. 21, 1738
Samuel Karney	Sept. 7, 1741	Cornelius McColgan	Aug. 21, 1759
Mary Kearn	Aug. 7, 1749	Samuel McCollin	Dec. 10, 1725
Margaret Keene	Dec. 30, 1759	Mary McCollister	Mar. 18, 1731
John Keeny	Apr. 25, 1742	Elizabeth McCollister	Dec. 20, 1736
Richard Kelley	Oct. 15, 1731	Henry McCollogh	Nov. 21, 1740
Mary, daughter of		John McComb	Sept. 10, 1723
Patrick Kenedy	June 30, 1753	Andrew McCullah	July 4, 1752
Mary Kenney	July 15, 1745	James McCullough	May 13, 1750
Elizabeth Kenoby	Mar. 11, 1748	John McDaniel	Nov. 1, 1755
John Kern	Mar. 29, 1759	Mary, wife of	
Austatia Kerney	Aug. 29, 1716	Cornelius McDaniel	Aug. 27, 1759
Samuel Kerrye	Nov. 22, 1718	John McDowell	Oct. 17, 1738
Elizabeth Kilpatrick	July 16, 1734	Anne McDowell	Sept. 17, 1739
Joseph Kirwan	July 4, 1710	John McGee	Mar. 18, 1733
Michael Koyl	Sept. 28, 1749	Catherine McEvers	Dec. 20, 1753
Seth Koyle	July 10, 1752	John McMahon	Mar. 30, 1758
Patrick Ladwell	Dec. 14, 1720	Agnes McMehin	Oct. 16, 1733
Robert Landy	Aug. 25, 1746	Elizabeth McMehin	Aug. 14, 1734
Elizabeth Leary	June 21, 1750	Francis Maccoy	July 23, 1746
Joseph Liney	July 1, 1738	Rebecca, wife of	
Michael Linney	Apr. 27, 1727	Timothy Mackarty	May 11, 1712
Joseph Linney	Oct. 10, 1734	Charles Mackarty	May 18, 1714
Samuel Linney	June 25, 1739	Elizabeth, wife of	
Peter Linney	May 23, 1755	William Mackmahon	Feb. 12, 1712
Edward Loughlen	Sept. 9, 1741	John Mackrel	July 13, 1745
John Lynch	Aug. 10, 1747	Anne Mackrell	Aug. 9, 1735
—— McCanin	Dec. 8, 1732	Jane Magee	Nov. 25, 1729

Name.	Date.	Name.	Date.
Margaret Magee	Aug. 8, 1743	James Neel	Sept. 14, 1722
Henry Magee	Aug. 18, 1744	Thompson Neugent	July 22, 1745
William Magee	Feb. 16, 1756	Mary Nevil	May 18, 1727
James Magee	May 4, 1759	Thomas Nevill	Sept. 15, 1730
Thomas Magee	Oct. 11, 1759	Anne Neville	Oct. 10, 1759
George Maggee	June 28, 1745	Matthew Newel	Mar. 1, 1712
Thomas Manerin		Matthew Newel	Apr. 9, 1744
"from Dublin"	June 24, 1735	Ann Newel	Oct. 29, 1751
Margaret Maney	Jan. 15, 1752	Alice, daughter of	
Anne Manny	Sept. 5, 1738	Bryan O'Neal	Sept. 2, 1736
Mary Manny	July 10, 1756	Mary, daughter of	
Anne, daughter of		William Oborne	Mar. 15, 1731
Daniel Mare	Sept. 30, 1751	Mary, daughter of	
John Meakins	Jan. 19, 1741	William O'Bourne	Dec. 28, 1732
Sarah Meakins	Mar. 12, 1747	Timothy Penney	Jan. 14, 1752
Robert Meakins	May 17, 1747	S. Phagan	Mar. 6, 1723
Thomas Mekins	Sept. 2, 1734	Frances Phin	Oct. 7, 1747
Thomas Miles	May 22, 1720	Martha Pigot	July 13, 1748
Elizabeth Miles	May 25, 1759	Elizabeth Plunket	Nov. 14, 1748
John Mitchel	Dec. 18, 1725	Jane Power	Dec. 15, 1729
Susannah Mitchel	Oct. 16, 1737	Catherine Quin	Aug. 19, 1741
Anne Mitchel	Nov. 13, 1748	Jane Quirke	May 12, 1718
—— Mooney	Mar. 15, 1746	Michael Reddiford	Nov. 1, 1734
Humphrey Morey	Nov. 21, 1722	John Redding	Sept. 8, 1738
James Morrison	Sept. 2, 1752	Jane Reily	June 18, 1759
Elizabeth Morrison	June 9, 1753	Robert Reyley	June 26, 1751
Martha, wife of Dennis		Hannah, wife of	
Mulholland	Feb. 23, 1744	Edward Reyley	Dec. 11, 1752
Catherine Mullen	Dec. 2, 1750	John Rial	Dec. 15, 1726
Mary Mullin	Oct. 16, 1744	John Riall	Sept. 23, 1739
Anne Mullin	Jan. 15, 1754	John Riley	Nov. 24, 1718
Elizabeth, wife of		Penelope Roache	Feb. 26, 1715
Nicholas Murphew	Aug. 20, 1757	Sarah Ryal	Aug. 2, 1746
Katherine Murphy	Aug. 23, 1745	Mary Ryal	Aug. 7, 1746
——, daughter of		Jane Ryal	Aug. 17, 1746
Bartholomew Murphy	Aug. 9 1756	Mary Ryal	Aug. 5, 1748
Richard Murrow	Aug. 8, 1714	David Ryal	Oct. 31, 1748
Mary Myhill	Sept. 25, 1727	William Rayll	Nov. 27, 1732
John Neal	June 29, 1729	Jane Ryall	Dec. 4, 1743
Susannah Neal	July 8, 1734	Martha Ryan	Dec. 6, 1748
Henry Neal	July 8, 1734	Sarah, daughter of	
Isabella Neal	July 19, 1746	Luke Scanlan	Oct. 12, 1759
Sarah Neal	Oct. 16, 1748	Elinor, wife of	
John Neal	July 21, 1759	Edward Shea	Sept. 11, 1748
Margaret Nealson	Oct. 8, 1754	Robert Strahan	July 30, 1741

Name.	Date.	Name.	Date.
Margaret Sulivan	Sept. 7, 1749	Geo. Welsh	Feb. 2, 1714
Dennis Sullivan	Aug. 28, 1757	Hannah Whelin	Feb. 27, 1731
Thomas Taife	Nov. 3, 1752	Samuel Welsh	Jan. 1702
Mary Tally	Sept. 20, 1759		

In addition to these, there is a large number of Moores, Whites and Browns on the burial records. One of the most prominent families buried in Christ Churchyard are the Conynghams, descendants of Redmond Conyngham of Letterkenny, Ireland, who came to Philadelphia in 1756 and was one of the original members of the firm of J. M. Nesbit and Company, an old house which greatly distinguished itself during the American Revolution.

EARLY PITTSBURGH, PENNSYLVANIA.

BY MICHAEL J. O'BRIEN.

In the Colonial days, the present site of the city of Pittsburgh, or a large part of it, was occupied by Forts Pitt and Duquesne, two historic frontier posts which were the scenes of many conflicts between the white men and the redskins. One of the first white men mentioned in the history of this region was the noted Indian trader, George Croghan, a native of County Sligo. Ireland, who is referred to frequently in the Colonial manuscripts of New York and Pennsylvania, and who was the father of Colonel George Croghan, the heroic defender of Fort Stephenson in the second war for independence.

The original name of the present flourishing city was "The Manor of Pittsburgh." In 1783, its proprietors, John Penn, Senior, and John Penn, Junior, announced a sale of the lands comprising the Manor and the first sale was made in January, 1784, to Major James Craig and Stephen A. Bayard of all the ground between Fort Pitt and the Allegheny River, supposed to contain about three acres. The plot included the ground now bounded by Penn Avenue, Third Street and the two rivers. Afterwards, it passed into the possession of Colonel James O'Hara and upon the division of the O'Hara estate in the year 1827, it fell to his daughter, Mrs. Mary Croghan. From her it passed to her daughter, Mary E. Croghan, who married a Captain

Schenley of London in 1841. The property is now known as the Schenley estate.

In Killikelly's "History of Pittsburgh," Craig and O'Hara are described as among the very first permanent settlers of Fort Pitt and the first who purchased lands there with the intention of making the place their home. "To these two and a very few others," says Killikelly, "belongs the honor of the title, 'The Founders of Pittsburgh.'" Craig emigrated from Ireland to Philadelphia in 1767 and at the outbreak of the Revolution became a captain of marines. Later, he became a captain of artillery and served throughout the war. Toward the close of the war, he was ordered to Pittsburgh and thereafter continued to make it his home. He filled many offices of public trust and took an active part in the development of the town. O'Hara was a man of education and parts. He emigrated from Ireland to Philadelphia in 1772 and became interested almost immediately in the Indian trade and in the Western country. He served throughout the Revolutionary War and came to Pittsburgh in 1783, and built his home on the Allegheny River above Fort Pitt. During the Indian campaigns of Generals Harmar, St. Clair and Wayne, he was an extensive contractor of supplies for the army, and in 1792 was appointed Quarter-master General of the United States Army. He was also largely engaged in the manufacture of salt and purchased extensive tracts of land in and about Pittsburgh, which have been the foundations of several great fortunes of to-day. General O'Hara was actively interested in almost every enterprise in connection with the young town and was one of its foremost citizens. He died in 1819. The historian of Pittsburgh asserts that the place "owed more to General James O'Hara for her prestige as a commercial and manufacturing centre in its pioneer days than to any other one man." He and Craig began the first glass works in Pittsburgh in 1797.

But, long before this time, there are records of Irish people in this vicinity. Reverend Father Lambing of Lancaster, a noted Pennsylvania historian, and founder of *American Catholic Historical Researches*, in one of the early issues of that excellent quarterly\ published the "Registres des Baptesmes et Sepultres," kept by Father Denys Baron, who, in 1756, was chaplain of French soldiers at Fort Duquesne. From these I take the following extracts: "L'an mille sept cent cinquante six le quinze de May a est baptisée par nous pretre Recolet soussigné aumonier du Roy au fort Duquesne sous le titre de l'Assomption de la Ste. Vierge à la belle Rivière et cela avec les ceremonies de la Ste. Église Helaine Condon agée de deux mois, fille de Jean Condon et de Sara Choisy, ses pére et mère en legitime mariage tous deux irlandois de nation et catholiques de Religion, lesquels ont etépris par le Chaouoinons en venant ici se joindre aux catholiques."

Translating this, it says: "In the year one thousand seven hundred and fifty-six, on the 15th of May, was baptized by us, Recollect Priest, the undersigned Chaplain of the King at Fort Duquesne, under the title of the Assumption of the Blessed Virgin, at the Beautiful River, and that with the ceremonies of the Holy Church, Ellen Condon, aged two months, the daughter of John Condon and of Sarah Choisy, the father and mother being united in lawful wedlock, both being Irish Catholics who were captured by the Shawnees in coming here to join the Catholics." The baptismal certificate was signed jointly by the sponsors, the father of the child and the officiating priest.

Other similar entries on the Registers are: Baptism of Mary Louisa, daughter of Patrick Flarcy and Frances Langford, "both Irish Catholics," also captured by the Indians, on July 9th, 1756. On August 10th, 1756, Catherine Smith was baptized. She was of English parentage and the godfather was "John Hannigan, an Irishman and a Catholic," and the godmother, "Barbara Conrad, a German and a Catholic." On the 18th of the same month, John Turner was baptised. The sponsors were John Hannigan and "Sarah Foissy, an Irishwoman and a Catholic."

ANOTHER EARLY RECORD OF PITTSBURGH, PA.

PUBLISHED BY THE PENNSYLVANIA HISTORICAL SOCIETY.

From "A list of the number of men, women and children not belonging to the army," at Fort Pitt on July 27, 1760.

Hugh McSwine	William McAllister
James Braden	William Bryan
Philip Boyle	John McKee
William Splane	William Downey

James Milligan
John Finley
John McCluer
Thomas Walsh
James Cahoon
Patrick Cunningham
John Dily
Charles Boyle
Thomas McCollum
Patrick Feagan
John Sinnott
Philip Sinnott

Neil McCollum
Patrick McCarty
John Coleman
Charles Hayes
Susannah McSwaine
George McSwaine
Mary McSwaine
Lydia McCarty
Margaret Coghran
Susan Daily
Rebecca Doyle
Margaret Doyle

From "A return of the number of houses, of the names of the owners and number of men, women and children at Fort Pitt on April 14, 1761."

John Welch
Thomas Kalhoun
Thomas Mitchell
Dennis Dogarty
Hugh McSwine
John Finley
Richard McMahan
James Meligan
John Hart
George Croghan
Philip Boyle
William McCallaster
Thomas Camey
John Cusick
John Sutton

Charles Boyle
Patrick McQuaid
Hugh Read
Robert Read
William Splane
Neil McCollom
Dennis McGlaulin
John Neal
Dennis Hall
Patrick McCarty
James Gilbey
John Dayley
Joseph McMurray
Michael McMurray
William Cassaday

EARLY IMMIGRANTS TO VIRGINIA (1623 to 1666) COL-
LECTED BY GEORGE CABELL GREER, CLERK,
VIRGINIA STATE LAND OFFICE, FROM THE
RECORDS OF THE LAND OFFICE, IN RICHMOND.

COMMUNICATED BY MICHAEL J. O'BRIEN.

Patrick Allen, 1653.
Teague Allen, 1653.
Peter Bandon, 1654.
Richard Banen, 1635.
Richard Barogan, 1653.
Henry Barrett, 1652.
Jane Barrett, 1652.
Symon Barrett, 1652.
Richard Barrett, 1653.
Sara Barrett, 1649.
Michael Barrow, 1653.
Garratt Barry, 1651.
Richard Boyle, 1638.
Darby Browne, 1654.
Teague Bryan, 1649.
Garret Bryan, 1653.
Humphrey Buckley, 1639.
Richard Buckley, 1637.
Arthur Buckley, 1647.
Ann Burk, 1647.
Charles Cain, 1654.
Charles Callahan, 1637.
John Cannaday, 1642.
Cornelius Canedy, 1650.
Cornelius Candia, 1652.
Bryan Candia, 1654.
Patrick Candell, 1637.
John Cane, 1637.
Robert Canlly, 1637.
Danny Carbry, 1656.
Thomas Caresy, 1650.
Thomas Caresy, 1654.
William Carney, 1650.

David Carrell, 1653.
Elizabeth Carrill, 1638.
Mahan Carty, 1655.
Bridget Carey, 1654.
Edward Carey, 1654.
Thomas Carey, 1653.
William Carey, 1653.
John Carey, 1653.
Richard Casey, 1636.
Richard Casey, 1637.
Patrick Cane, 1639.
James Clansey, 1638.
Patrick Clarke, 1650.
Brian Clarke, 1652.
Patrick Clark, 1655.
Thomas Clary, 1642.
Thomas Clarye, 1653.
Patrick Closse, 1641.
John Coffey, 1637.
Thomas Coggin, 1642.
Sarah Coggin, 1638.
John Coheane, 1653.
Francis Cogun, 1653.
Thomas Colran, 1635.
John Conady, 1652.
John Conden, 1638.
John Connaway, 1638.
Jeremiah Connaway, 1642.
Nicholas Connaway, 1651.
Henry Connaway, 1652.
Martha Connaway, 1652.
Aron Conway, 1642.
Philip Conner, 1638.

Dennes Conner, 1652.
Richard Conniers, 1654.
Thomas Coniers, 1654.
Robert Corbett, 1635.
Ann Corbett, 1651.
Edward Cotterell, 1635.
Ambrose Cotterell, 1649.
Michael Crawley, 1641.
Patrick Cugley, 1650.
Katharine Cullaine, 1653.
Joane Cullin, 1652.
Joane Cullin, 1642.
Katherine Cullins, 1635.
Alice Curley, 1636.
James Daley, 1646.
George Daley, 1655.
William Dally, 1655.
Owen Daltie, 1655.
John Dalton, 1652.
John Dalton, 1654.
John Dellony, 1654.
John Denaley, 1654.
Shela Dennis, 1654.
Stephen Donaway, 1654.
Mary Donellin, 1655.
Thomas Donellin, 1655.
Martin Donifin, 1637.
Thomas Dowde, 1656.
Edmund Dowland, 1654.
Peter Dowland, 1650.
Francis Dowling, 1643.
Robert Dunn, 1650.
Thomas Dunne, 1650.
Patrick Farrell, 1638.
Garrett Farrell, 1637.
Alexander Farrell, 1656.
Garrett Farrell, 1638.
John Farrahoe, 1645.
Katherine Ferrell, 1649.

Redmond Fitzgarret, 1635.
James Flaharty, ——.
James Flaherty, 1651.
Teague Flanny, 1655.
Patrick Flemin, 1652.
Eliza Fleming, 1650.
Christopher Fleming, 1653.
Richard Fleming, 1643.
John Fleming, 1653.
Teague Fleming, 1655.
John Fling, 1638.
Patrick Forgeson, 1652.
Francis Gargen, 1653.
Richard Gayney, 1655.
Robert Gayney, 1654.
Conner Gilleailow, 1655.
Henry Gillingham, 1642.
George Gillin, 1638.
Daniel Gillins, 1650.
Alexander Grogan, 1652.
James Haley, 1654.
Ann Haley, 1654.
Patrick Harper, 1653.
Teague Hart, 1655.
Anthony Hayes, 1643.
Robert Hayes, 1642.
Francis Hayes, 1653.
Alexander Hayes, 1654.
Edward Hayes, 1653.
Eliza Hayes, 1651.
Ann Hayes, 1643.
Mary Hayes, 1643.
Mary Hayes, 1654.
Peter Hayes, 1637.
Richard Hayes, 1635.
David Hayes, 1638.
Mary Hayes, 1637.
William Hayes, 1638.
Henry Hayes, 1638.

Richard Heady, 1654.
Robert Hearne, 1652.
Thomas Hearne, 1639.
Thomas Hearne, 1650.
John Hearne, 1639.
John Hearne, 1636.
Humphrey Heggins, 1652.
John Hely, 1643.
John Hely, 1637.
Robert Hely, 1635.
William Hely, 1637.
Roger Hengan, 1649.
William Heyley, 1635.
Francis Heynes, 1653.
Thomas Heynes, 1654.
John Higgins, 1639.
Dan Higgins, 1654.
Jone Higgins, 1638.
John Higgins, 1639.
Francis Higgins, 1651.
Darby Howranley, 1656.
Thomas Hynes, 1637.
Sarah Hynes, 1640.
John Joice, 1637.
Peter Joice, 1652.
Robert Joyce, 1637.
John Joyce, 1635.
John Joyce, 1637.
Giles Joyce, 1654.
John Joyce, 1650.
Martin Joyce, 1650.
Mary Joyce, 1652.
Patrick Jordan, 1655.
Philip Kahan, 1655.
James Kaiton, 1652.
Hester Kasey, 1638.
William Kayne, 1654.
Sarah Keelin, 1638.
Alice Kelly, 1651.

Elizabeth Kelly, 1652.
Thomas Kelly, 1652.
Abraham Kelly, 1643.
Bryan Kelly, 1638.
Bryan Kelly, 1636.
James Kenney, 1642.
Roger Kenney, 1638.
Richard Kenny, 1637.
Edward Kenny, 1655.
Edmund Kenny, 1655.
David Kerney, 1654.
Nicholas Keytin, 1639.
Karbury Kigon, 1643.
Charles Kiggon, 1651.
John Keynan, 1655.
Arthur Lahey, 1649.
William Larkin, 1654.
Elizabeth Larkin, 1654.
Richard Lary, 1635.
Thomas Laughlin, 1654.
Jeremiah Lynch, 1638.
John Macalester, 1654.
John Macdonell, 1650.
William Mackgahaye, 1653.
Pat Mac-Manor, 1653.
John Mack Maroe, 1655.
John Mackan, 1652.
Oneal Mackdoneal, 1655.
Thomas Mackdonell, 1653.
Dan Mackdonell, 1653.
Neale Mackee, 1652.
James MacKeney, 1656.
William MackKenly, 1653.
Dennis Mackernall, 1655.
John Macknillian, 1655.
—— Mackinellan, 1656.
James Mackniel 1652.
John Mackneall, 1648.
Patrick Mackroe, 1653.

Owen Macurt, 1655.
Henry Maddin, 1643.
Owen Madrin, 1640.
Richard Magee, 1642.
John Magee, 1635.
Charles Maguiry, 1653.
Dennis Mahonney, 1635.
David Mahoone, 1656.
Daniel Maley, 1647.
Cormack Malloy, 1655.
Patrick Manough, 1653.
James Marfey (Murphy), 1637.
Mary Morfey (Murphy), 1650.
Michaell Morphew (Murphy)
1639.
Edward Murferry (Murphy)
1649.
John Marogan, 1651.
Katherine Mecane, 1655.
Dan Macannick, 1653.
Hugh Michalla, 1650.
John Michallen, 1654.
Elisa Macartee, 1653.
Dennis Molocklan, 1656.
William Monahan, 1654.
Thomas Moone, (y), 1652.
Henry Moone, 1652.
John Moone, 1647.
Susan Moone, 1635.
Arthur Moone, 1652.
Dermot Morane, 1655.
Edward Moyle, 1654.
Roger Moyle, 1654.
Andrew Muher, 1654.
Thomas Mullett, 1653.
John Mullins, 1652.
Teague Nealy, 1655.
William Newgent, 1654.
C——— Newgent, 1635.

Christopher Nugent, 1638.
Daniel Odaley, 1656.
Richard O'Kell, 1654.
Patt O'Mallin, 1651.
Daniel O'Melle, 1656.
Thomas Ororke, 1652.
Margaret Osheelivan, 1654.
Teague Owen, 1655.
Dan O'Carbry, 1655.
Patrick O'Crahan, 1656.
John O'Drenne, 1655.
Thomas O'Derrick, 1655.
——— O'Fahee, 1655.
Teague O'Fallon, 1656.
Dermot O'Farne, 1656.
Farell O'Gley, 1656.
Donell O'Graham, 1655.
John O'Grangenes, 1655.
Richard O'Harrott, 1655.
Richard O'Harrough, 1655.
Nella O'Lanny, 1656.
Owin O'Leaby, 1655.
John O'Leally, 1656.
Jane O'Lire, 1656.
G——— O'Loffe, 1656.
Thomas O'Lyn, 1655.
Cormack O'Mally, 1655.
Connor O'Morpher, 1655.
Teague O'Maulins, 1655.
William O'Naught, 1655.
John O'William, 1656.
Patrick Paul, 1648.
Phillipp Prendergast, 1643.
Philip Prendergast, 1647.
Philip Prendergast, 1655.
Joane Qually, 1653.
Thomas Reley, 1654.
Richard Riley, 1649.
Patrick Robinson, 1637.

James Roche, 1637.
John Roche, 1647.
Teague Row, 1655.
Ann Ryley, 1653.
Thomas Sherridon, 1642.
Richard Sexton, 1653.
Nicholas Sexton, 1654.
John Sheeles, 1653.
Ellen Sheen, 1650.
Roger Sheely, 1656.
Teague Shone, 1655.
Daniel Shullivan, 1656.
Dorman Shullivan, 1656.
Elinor Silivean, 1653.
Peter Sharkey, 1649.
Peter Starkey, 1652.
Philip Starkey, 1652.
William Starkey, 1652.
Patrick Steward, 1655.
Onory Sullivan, 1656.
Elizabeth Sullivant, 1655.
Edmund Sweny, 1656.
Elizabeth Sweney, 1656.
Mary Sweney, 1656.
Cornelius Swillivon, 1637.

Joane Taaffee, 1654
Eliza Talley, 1638.
Eliza Talley, 1636.
Patrick Tallin, 1652.
Patrick Talling, 1638.
William Tandey, 1650.
William Tandy, 1643.
Brian Teagee, 1655.
Dennis Teague, 1655.
John Toole, 1655.
Thomas Toolye, 1638.
Thomas Tooly, 1654.
Robert Tracye, 1653.
Mary Tracy, 1654.
Robert Tracy, 1653.
Teague Trassey, 1655.
Robert Trasey, 1654.
John Tulley, 1640.
James Turney, 1652.
Patrick Vaughan, 1635.
Patrick Vaughan, 1638.
Thomas Walsh, 1643.
Thomas Welsh, 1638.
Robert Welshe, 1635.
Patrick White, 1653.

In addition to these, there is a large number of immigrants named Allen, Bryan, Collins, Cunningham, Donnell, Farley, Flood, Fludd, Ford, Foard, Gill, Gray, Garrett, Griffin, Gwyn, Hart, Haies, Harrington, Moore, and Neale who may have been Irish.

GRANTEES OF LANDS IN THE COLONY AND STATE OF VIRGINIA—
COPIED FROM THE COUNTY RECORDS OF VIRGINIA.

BY MICHAEL J. O'BRIEN.

These are not all claimed as Irish, for, as a matter of fact, as far as I know, there is no reference on the records to the nationality of many of these people. As is well known, there are some family names that are common to Ireland, England and Scotland and when the place of nativity or the descent is not stated it is not always possible to determine what the nationality of the early American settlers may have been. Names like Collins, Moore, Hayes, Gill, Ford, Griffin, Harrington, Farley and so on, are common in Irish nomenclature, but, so are they in English nomenclature, and such names are met with frequently in England. It is possible, therefore, that some of these people were of English origin.

Year.	Name.	Number of Acres.	In What County.
1628	Walter Heyley	50	Elizabeth City
1634	William Conner	50	Elizabeth City
1635	Thomas Keeling	100	Elizabeth City
1636	Joseph Moore	200	Elizabeth City
1638	Bryan Smith	140	Westmoreland
1639	Christopher Dawcey	50	Elizabeth City
1646	John Flynn	50	Westmoreland
1647	Francis Fludd	300	Westmoreland
1649	Thomas Conniers	40	Elizabeth City
1650	George Gill	700	Westmoreland
1650	John Haney	950	Northumberland
1651	Christopher Boyce	300	Northumberland
1651	Stephen Gill	900	Northumberland
1651	John Hayes	300	Westmoreland
1653	Charles Kiggan	100	Westmoreland
1651	Abraham Moore and Thomas Griffin	1400	Lancaster
1653	Dennis Conniers	1417	Lancaster
1653	Patrick Miller	400	Lancaster
1653	Hugh Gwynn	200	Lancaster
1653	Teague Floyne	300	Lancaster
1652	Daniel Welch	1137	Lancaster
1652	Anthony Doney	1000	Lancaster
1654	Edwin Connaway	1250	Lancaster
1656	Dennis Conniers	1178	Lancaster
1658	Henry Roach	1700	Westmoreland

Year	Name.	Number of Acres.	In What County
1658	John Kenneygan and James Fullerton	458	Rappahannock
1658	William Goffe	1000	New Kent
1661	John Fleming	493	New Kent
1663	Peter Ford	640	New Kent
1664	Cornelius Reynolds	640	New Kent
1664	John Goffe	400	New Kent
1663	Miles Riley	200	Rappahannock
1663	Dennis Sullivant	1446	Rappahannock
1664	James Caghill	246	Rappahannock
1662	John Rayney	1178	Lancaster
1663	Daniel Welch	600	Lancaster
1663	Thomas Crily	600	Accomac
1664	William O'Naughton and Teague Miskett	400	Accomac
1664	John Renny	500	Accomac
1665	Edward Haelly	1000	Elizabeth City
1665	Miles Reily	1100	Rappahannock
1666	Dorman Sullivant	500	Accomac
1666	William Onoughton	500	Accomac
1667	Ambrose Cleare	1155	Rappahannock
1667	John Lacey	370	Rappahannock
1668	Francis Haile	1865	Rappahannock
1668	John Sexton	700	New Kent
1669	Martyn Moore	400	Accomac
1669	Thomas Orily	300	Accomac
1669	Bickett Burke	408	Rappahannock
1669	Cornelius Reynolds	180	Gloucester
1669	Thomas Collins	250	Gloucester
1670	Thomas Moore	2400	Isle of Wight
1672	Ambrose White	450	Accomac
1672	Augustine Moore	225	Elizabeth City
1670	Edward Reyley and John Killingham	500	Rappahannock
1670	John Butler	597	Rappahannock
1670	Christopher Butler	339	Rappahannock
1672	Henry Tandy	868	Rappahannock
1673	Thomas Ryland	120	Gloucester
1674	Daniel Sullivant and Theophilus Wale	450	Rappahannock
1675	Bryan Smith	2200	Rappahannock
1675	Thomas Heady	475	Accomac
1678	Malachi Peal	843	Elizabeth City
1678	John Quigley	80	Elizabeth City
1679	William Collins	1313	Isle of Wight

Year.	Name.	Number of Acres.	In What County.
1681	Edwin Conway	1200	Rappahannock
1681	John Moore	300	Isle of Wight
1682	Morris Mackashannock	140	Gloucester
1682	Daniel Long	60	Isle of Wight
1682	William Hogin	15	Gloucester
1683	Cornelius Reynolds	300	Rappahannock
1683	David Condon	114	York
1684	Bryan Moore and John Cochlen	200	York
1684	John Corbett	700	Gloucester
1685	P. Dunn	146	Elizabeth City
1684	John Piggot	374	Henrico
1684	James Tullagh	274	Isle of Wight
1686	Matthew Tomlin	1227	Isle of Wight
1686	Henry Hearne	266	Isle of Wight
1687	Thomas Moore	1150	Isle of Wight
1688	Peter Butler, John Butler and James Butler	678	Isle of Wight
1688	Alexander Mackenny	296	Henrico
1690	Hugh Owen	220	Rappahannock
1690	Cornelius Nowell	390	Rappahannock
1691	Richard Kennon and others	2827	Henrico
1691	William Fleming	600	Gloucester
1691	William Collaine	140	Gloucester
1691	William Collins and Timothy Conniers	620	King and Queen
1693	Owen Davis	193	York
1694	John MacKenny	450	Isle of Wight
1695	Owen Daniel	130	Isle of Wight
1693	William Collaline	97	Gloucester
1694	Francis Mackenny	180	Accomac
1695	Dennis Morris	300	Richmond
1698	James Whaley	200	York
1698	Daniel Gowin	52	Gloucester
1701	Charles Fleming	493	King and Queen
1702	Barnaby Mackinnie	308	Isle of Wight
1704	John Gill	235	Henrico
1704	Daniel McCarty	1350	Rappahannock
1704	John Tarpley	100	Rappahannock
1704	William Callawne	62	Gloucester
1705	Timothy Conner	1420	King and Queen
1712	Edward Fagan	150	Rappahannock
1714	Bryan Foley	250	Rappahannock
1714	Henry Gill	500	Henrico
1716	John Doyle	226	Rappahannock
1715	Daniel Malone	99	Prince George

Year.	Name.	Number of Acres.	In What County.
1715	Patrick Grady	250	Richmond
1715	Christopher Marr	171	Richmond
1717	Mary Doyle	249	Richmond
1717	Richard Dearden	100	Prince George
1717	Richard Tally	181	Prince George
1717	William Kennon	42	Henrico
1717	John Tally	300	Prince George
1716	Michael Ginings and John Sutton	200	King and Queen
1718	Mark Moore	500	Henrico
1719	Lawrence Butler	597	Richmond
1722	Daniel Croom	400	Henrico
1722	Dennis Connyers	840	King George
1724	Michael Meldrum	635	King George
1725	Thomas Welch	1267	King George
1726	Edward Newgent	322	King George
1726	Jeremiah Murdock	362	King George
1727	Daniel Maher	841	King George
1728	Patrick Mullin	350	Goochland
1729	Nicholas Cox	400	Goochland
1729	James Nevil	800	Goochland
1729	Neil McCormick	42	King George
1730	Owen Grinan	119	King George
1730	Michael Holland and William Ford	400	Goochland
1730	Thomas Murrell	400	Goochland
1731	Stephen Lacey	800	Goochland
1731	Matthew Cox	400	Goochland
1731	Charles Rayley	394	Goochland
1731	John Cunningham	400	Goochland
1731	Alexander Logan	400	Goochland
1732	Agnes Noland	354	Goochland
1732	Samuel Burke	200	Goochland
1734	John Casey	62	Elizabeth City
1733	Charles Lynch	800	Goochland
1734	Thomas Murrell	71	Goochland
1734	John Cunningham	200	Goochland
1737	Hugh Rea	118	Caroline
1740	Thomas Collins	90	Caroline
1754	William Flood	153	Richmond
1754	Redmond Follin	1080	Halifax
1755	David Hailey	207	Halifax
1755	William Gill	400	Halifax
1754	James Machan	510	Halifax
1754	Daniel Daly	400	Halifax

Year.	Name.	Number of Acres.	In What County.
1756	Charles Macceney	124	Cumberland
1755	James Cain	28	Sussex
1755	Thomas Clary	67	Sussex
1757	Ambrose Haley	386	Halifax
1758	Michael McDaniel	820	Halifax
1759	Timothy Dalton	150	Halifax
1758	William Raney	250	Dinwiddie
1758	Joseph Butler	120	Dinwiddic
1758	Anne Fitzgerald	182	Dinwiddic
1760	Richard Murphey	400	Halifax
1760	William McDaniel	1000	Halifax
1760	Richard Griffin	394	Halifax
1760	Hugh Moore	800	Halifax
1760	James Careley	400	Halifax
1760	William Carley	170	Halifax
1760	Morris Dunn	190	Sussex
1760	William Dillon	250	Cumberland
1761	Anthony Griffin	244	Halifax
1761	Hugh Corrin	424	Halifax
1761	Richard Dugen	660	Halifax
1761	John Logan	383	Halifax
1761	Henry McDaniel	285	Halifax
1762	Darby Callihan	400	Halifax
1762	Christopher Gorman	294	Halifax
1762	Richard Griffin	400	Halifax
1762	Martin Burk	100	Cumberland
1763	Jeremiah Morrow	260	Halifax
1764	William O'Bannon	258	Faquier
1764	David Logan	217	Halifax
1764	William Mead	185	Halifax
1764	Owen Brady	400	Halifax
1764	John Butler	835	Halifax
1764	Thomas Collins	400	Halifax
1764	Edward Cahall	217	Halifax
1764	William McDaniel	299	Halifax
1765	Thomas Dougherty	400	Halifax
1765	Ambrose Haley	275	Halifax
1765	Patrick Shields	51	Halifax
1767	Thomas Conner	348	Halifax
1767	John Fitzgerald	400	Halifax
1770	Thomas Barrett	28	Dinwiddie
1770	James Foley	117	Faquier
1772	William Connelly	210	Sussex
1772	Peter Cain	244	Sussex
1773	John Connolly	2000	Fincastle

Year.	Name.	Number of Acres.	In What County.
1780	William Conway	70	Faquier
1783	John Kelley	50	Sussex
1783	Michael Molone	5¾	Sussex
1785	Thomas Creagh	150	Sussex
1788	James Dowdall	586	Faquier
1791	Michael Malone	131	Sussex
1794	Peter Conway	31	Faquier
1795	James Lyon	120	Sussex
1796	Joseph Reynolds	209	Sussex
1796	John Dillian	40	Sussex
1797	Michael Ahart	147	Sussex
1798	John Kelley	66	Faquier

EXTRACTS FROM THE VIRGINIA MARRIAGE RECORDS.

BY MICHAEL J. O'BRIEN.

There is a wealth of evidence in support of the claim that the Irish settled in large numbers in Virginia at an early date. No one has ever taken the trouble of writing these people down in history and the American Irish themselves have been too negligent to attend to it, so their story is lost for all time. In most cases, little or nothing remains but the mere mention of their names on the Colonial records. The Church and Land records are the best of these sources of information.

FAQUIER COUNTY.

Date.	Bridegroom.	Bride.
1765, February 11	James Neilson	Betty O'Banon
1766, April 24	John Foley	Milly Ashby
1768, October 25	Francis Atwell	Mary McDonald
1771, January 28	Isaac McCoy	Bridget Withers
1771, December 23	Joseph Nelson	Catherine O'Banon
1777, October 10	Andrew O'Bannon	Mary Smith
1777, July 28	Patrick Whalon	Susannah Leach
1777, March 24	John Dulin	Fanny Glascock
1777, May 5	William Berry	Clara Feagan
1777, January 2	Thomas Bartlett	Sarah Carroll
1777, May 17	George Berry	Sarah Conway
1780, December 10	John Nelson	Bathsheba Hogan
1780, May 23	John Brian	Mary Linn
1780, November 27	Elisha Harris	Margaret McCormick
1780, November 23	Benjamin O'Banon	Eleanor Ash

Date.	Bridegroom.	Bride.
1781, September 24	John Murphew	Joan Waddell
1781, December 14	Henry Allen	Catherine McKonkey
1781, May 22,	Robert McMehin	Patty Russell
1782, August 26	Samuel Singleton	Mary Ann Connelly
1782, September 2	Joseph Obanon	Elizabeth Grigsby
1783, January 21	Thomas Obanon	Hannah Barker
1783, September 19	John Hailey	Peggy Jett
1783, June 14	James Healey	Lucy Jeffries
1785, September 28	Daniel Cummins	Sarah Sullivan
1785, October 20	Epaphroditus Hubbard	Ann McCarthy
1785, November 23	William Kirkpatrick	Mary Feagan
1785, December 21	Benjamin Mahoney	Elizabeth Harriss
1785, January 12	William Malloney	Lucy Harrison
1785, August 24	John Roach	Patty McClanahan
1785, October 24	George Martin	Elizabeth MacCormack
1785, July 25	John Adams	Betsey McCormack
1786, March 13	John Larrance	Joyce O'Bannon
1786, June 3	David McClanahan	Elizabeth Fryer
1786, August 1	James Foley	Elizabeth Ogelby
1786, March 14	Levi Davis	Lydia Kearns
1786, August 28	George Foster	Sarah Conway
1786, May 2	Rawley Hogan	Peggy Conway
1786, November 30	Arch. Johnston	Jemima O'Banon
1786, August 26	Thomas Kerns	Mary Russell
1786, March 11	Abner Luttrell	Sarah Kelly
1786, December 18	John McCoy	Uriah Hickman
1787, September 24	James Callahan	Elizabeth Phillips
1787, April 19	Jesse Hinson	Mary Sullivan
1787, April 21	William McCoy	Nancy Kendall
1787, March 9	Joseph McCoy	Nancy Williams
1787, December 12	Cornelius McCarthy	Sukey Hardwick
1787, April 24	Thomas O'Neal	Esther Murray
1788, February 4	Alexander Brink	Mary Sullivan
1788, August 9	William Connor	Frankey Greening
1788, July 7	Joseph Conway	Sarah Turner
1788, January 28	Edward Dulin	Elizabeth Rhodes
1788, September 22	William Finnie	Lilly Collins
1788, March 24	Mason Lawrence	Nancy O'Banon
1788, September 29	William Welch	Lydia Congreve
1789, October 29	Daniel McLaren	Mary Todd
1789, January 10	Joseph Nay	Frances Mahoney
1789, February 18,	Abraham Parker	Priscilla McKoy
1789, April 29	William Tracey	Winny Grigsby
1789, January 26	James Garrett	Phebe Harley
1789, March 3	John Hansbrough	Sarah Lehogan
1789, December 26	Thomas Haney	Margaret Chappclear

Date.	Bridegroom.	Bride.
1789, December 23	Andrew Kenny	Nancy Horton
1789, June 27	Henry Logan	Hannah Kendall
1789, November 23	William McClanahan	Elizabeth Tillery
1789, August 25	Timothy Cunningham	Sarah Fishback
1789, September 8	Lewis Dulin	Ann Shud
1789, June 22	Edward Feagan	Polly Sinkler
1789, August 25	George Roach	Sarah White
1789, May 17	Thomas Dennahy	Ann Carter
1789, March 1	James Foley	Mary Bradford
1789, July 26	John Farrin	Lettice Riley
1790, October 22	Martin Covert	Susannah O'Bannon
1790, September 16	William Hailey	Susannah Jett
1790, April 21	John Humphries	Dorothy McConchie
1790, January 15	C. Magraw	Margaret Glasscock
1790, February 10	Daniel McCoy	Agnes Kamper
1790, October 20	Patrick Powers	Caty Snyder
1790, March 24	William Scott	Mary Ann Sullivan
1790, February 20	William Sullivan	Ann Jones
1790, November 16	William Murphy	Sally Bowen
1790, August 24	William H. McNeal	Elizabeth Kearns
1790, April 26	John Mackarel	Sally Morgan

NORFOLK COUNTY.

1728, February 14	Lazarus Sweeny	Elizabeth Wilson
1727, November 17	James Avery	Mary McNary
1738, July 4	James O'Bryan	Mary Langley
1735, ——	Alexander Bayne	Margaret Connor
1753, October 31	Roderick Conner	Margaret Scott
1754, April 23	John Walsh	Patience Davis
1757, January 20	Willis Dyson	Mary Conner
1758, August 21	William Moore	Betsey Bird
1758, September 29	James Murphree	Elizabeth Bratt
1760, December 4	John Dunn	Sarah Weatheradge
1762, July 26	Florence McNamara	Sarah Brodie
1762, September 2	Philip Carbery	Sarah Galt
1763, February 27	Daniel Gwyn	Mary Janes
1763, February 8	Arthur Boush	Ann Sweeney
1763, January 13	Christopher Busten	Elizabeth Dunn
1763, April 23	John Connor	Elizabeth Jening
1763, August 4	John McCarthy	Mary Avery
1764, March 29	Samuel Meade	Elizabeth McCurdy
1767, March 14	Charles Bushnell	Catherine McGee
1770, March 28	Thomas Burke	Mary Freeman
1770, March 21	Slaughter Cofield	Mary Carney
1773, February 17	David O'Sheal	Catherine Veale
1773, June 17	John Heffernan	Elizabeth Horton

Date.	Bridegroom.	Bride.
1773, August 11	Matthew Shields	Sarah Corprew
1774, August 3	Richard Carney	Sarah Lewwelling
1774, August 6	Michael Freadly	Mrs. McLochlen

GOOCHLAND COUNTY.

1783, April 21	Patrick Vaughan	Mary Smith
1781, August 30	David Mullins	Rosanna Herndon
1784, October 17	David Nowlin	Ann Powell
1787, November 27	David Carroll	Sally Carroll
1787, May 7	Richard McCary	Nancy Martin
1787, October 9	Daniel McCoy	Jane Parrish

YORK COUNTY.

1773, January 7	John Moss	Sarah Gibbons
1773, April 13,	John Richardson	Elizabeth Hayes
1775, May 23	Thomas Gibbons	Martha Lester
1776, March 4	Charles McFadden	Jane Lyppitit
1777, July 1	William Mallory	Martha Sweeney
1777, December 15	John McClary	Sarah Hansford
1778, April 16	John Glenn	Margaret Cunningham
1784, May 19	Wyatt Coleman	Mary Shields
1786, April 14	Warner Lewis	Sarah Shay
1792, August 20	Richard Toole	Ann Powers

LANCASTER COUNTY.

1719, August 24	Simon Shallard	Blanche Kelley
1724, May 5	Christopher Garlington	Elizabeth Conway
1724, September 22	Dennis McCarthy	Sarah Ball
1729, June 10	Robert Edmonds	Anne Conway
1732, August 19	Arthur McNeale	Elizabeth Frizzell
1736, January 15	John Cannaday	Katherine Heale
1745, April 6	William Kelly	Elizabeth Riley
1758, May 19	Thaddeus McCarty	Ann Chinn
1766, December 30	John Dunn	Caty McTyre

ELIZABETH CITY COUNTY.

1695, April 8	P. Dunn	Hannah Powers

SURREY COUNTY.

1779, September 8	Isham Inman	Mary Gibbons
1780, September 1	Samuel Thomas	Katherine Carrell

AMELIA COUNTY.

1749, January 26	Richard Burke	Milly Hawkins
1763, April 1	John Tabb	Mary Molloney
1786, January 24	Francis Fitzgerald	Mary Eppes
1786, September 28	Daniel Farley	Marietta Pryor

Date.	Bridegroom.	Bride.
1781, October 5	Harrison Jones	Ann Logan
1790, November 25	George Eggleston	Elizabeth Moran

ROCKBRIDGE AND AUGUSTA COUNTIES.

1785, December 6	Isaac Frenche	Margaret McCormick
1785, December 6	Arthur Connelly	Jane Dale
1786, January 12	Michael Kenady	Ellen McCafferty
1786, February 9	John Spence	Isabel McCormick
1786, March 13	Ephraim Doty	Ann Doherty
1789, January 22	James Talford	Jean McCorkery
1790, March 16	William Higginbottom	Polly Shannon
1790, July 31	John Doughady	Agnes Davidson
1790, December 8	Enoch Bogas	Elizabeth McCroskry
1792, May 29	Jacob Calk	Mary McFadden
1793, February 17	Daniel Moore	Martha Barrett

AUGUSTA COUNTY (*names of Bridegrooms, and dates only on record*).

1749, February	John McGill
1756, August	Patrick Miller
1758, July 20	Robert McMahon
1759, May 16	Edward McMullen
1760, January	Edward McGarry
1760, February	James McGaffock
1760, May	James McDowell
1762, March 18	Robert Murphy
1762, June 6	Thomas Rafferty
1762, June 6	Michael Cogen
1762, September 30	James McAffee
1765, October 17	William McBride
1766, June 20	Pat Christian
1766, September 10	Andrew Donelly
1769, December 26	William McClure
1770, January 24	John McClenahan
1770, April 10	Pat Buchanan
1770, October 3	Matthew Kenny
1770, December 5	Pat Lockhart

WESTMORELAND COUNTY.

1787, March 27	Edmund Bulger	Hannah Corbit Hudson
1787, August 22	John Wood	Molly Cahill
1787, November 8	John Murphy	Anna Ballantine
1788, January 10	Burwell Bassett	Eliza McCarty
1789, January 7	Edward Porter	Mary McClanahan
1789, March 17	John McKenny	Mary Sutton
1790, April 9	John Kirk	Elender McKenney
1790, December 11	Patrick Lynch	Deliby Dodd
1791, July 29	George McKenny	Elizabeth McGuire

Date.	*Bridegroom.*	*Bride.*
1791, January 5	John Locust	Sarah Kelly
1791, April 22	William Hutchings	Nancy Cavenaugh
1792, October 27	Youel Brennon	Sarah McKenney
1792, August 25	George Gregory	Ann Fitzgerald
1792, September 14	Peter Davis	Patty McGuire
1797, September 2	Daniel McCarty	Margaret Robinson
1798, February 21	Samuel Rust	Sary Clanahan
1799, December 30	James Mothershead	Elizabeth Riley
1800, October 27	Peter Gallagher	Betsey Garner

ORANGE COUNTY.

1770, October 3	Bernard Moore	Catherine Price
1790, January 28	John Furner	Sarah Fitzgerald
1790, July 31	John Donovan	Sally Gaer

NORTHUMBERLAND COUNTY.

1778, February 9	Nathaniel Brown	Nanny Dillon
1778, February 19	Thomas Butler	Frances Costin
1795, November 4	Moses Driskell	Margaret Joynes
1798, June 4	William Dillon	Nancy Fisher

SUSSEX COUNTY.

1765, June 20	Thomas Butler	Mary Norris
1768, February 28	William Biggins	Molly Biggins
1768, March 17	Lawrence Gibbons	Lucy Jones
1772, October 7	William Parham	Mary Kelley
1771, ——	Thomas Dunn	Sarah Hobbs
1771, ——	Thomas Chappell	Elizabeth Malone

CAROLINE COUNTY.

1770, September 8	John Chandler	Jenny McKee
1790, January 2	Thomas Donahoe	Patty Umbreckhouse
1795, January 6	William Collins	Elizabeth Pitts
1797, June 30	William Dunn	Sarah Coghill
1798, October 5	Henry Dunn	Ann Dunn

SPOTTSYLVANIA COUNTY.

1734, January 9	William Connor	Sarah Rogers
1739, May 13	James Dunn	Elinor Savage
1748, June 18	Patrick Connelly	Ann French
1797, March 15	John McKenny	Elizabeth Smith
1797, December 1	James McDermeath	Nancy Sutton
1798, December 24	Jesse Bradger	Frankey Sulliven
1798, ——	James Richason	Susanna McKenna
1798, December 24	Moses Burbridge	Fanny Haney

RICHMOND COUNTY.

1728, April 27	Thomas Beale	Sarah McCarty

FROM THE WILL BOOKS OF SPOTTSYLVANIA COUNTY.

Date.	Testator.	Witnesses.	Legatees.
1726, Dec. 6	James Sammis	John Corbet and John Nalle	
1732, Feby. 10	Ambrose Madison	Francis Conway	David Roach
1733, Sept. 4	Joel Johnson		Philemon Cavenaugh Sarah Cavenaugh Joel Cavenaugh
1734, June 4	John Davis	D. Byrne	
1735, Aug. 5	James Williams	John Conner	
1738, June 6	Timothy Coffey		
1744, Aug. 7		John Power	
1744, Aug. 7	John Talliaferro	Ann Power Sarah Power Susannah Power	
1744, Sept. 4	Edmund Byrne		Thomas Byrne of County Kildare, Ireland.
1748, Feby. 7	Thomas Collins	Thomas Collins William Collins John Collins	John Collins Edmund Collins
1754, May 7	Nicholas Hawkins		Cate Macdonel
1755, Feby. 5	Benjamin Mathews	Thomas McNeal	
1758, March 7	William Lynn		Daughter Hannah McCauley, the children of his brother Charles in Ireland and various relatives in Strabane and other parts of Ireland.
1766, Aug. 4	William Ellis		Ann O'Neal
1771, May 16	Elizabeth Battaley	Mildred Fitzsimmons	
1772, April 16	Ezekiah Ellis	Robert O'Neal	
1778, Sept. 17	Robert Chew	Thomas McGee	
1781, Oct. 18	William Dangerfield	Thomas Strahan	
1782, March 21	Ann Dansee	James Tobin	
1783, March 20	Benjamin Coyle	Michael Coyle	
1784, Feby. 19	Thomas McGee		
1786, Feby. 5	John Robinson	Elizabeth Kelley	
1789, Jany. 6	Francis Purvis	Michael McDonald	
1792, Feby. 7	Ann Gatewood	Mildred Delaney	

FROM ADMINISTRATION RECORDS OF SPOTTSYLVANIA COUNTY.

Date of Bond.	Deceased.	Administrator.
1727, May 2	Peter Kilgore	Mary Kilgore
1729, July 1	Samuel Wright	John Kilgore and Thomas Byrn
1733, April 3	Bryan Macleroy	Henry Willis
1739, Nov. 6	James Dunn	Ellinor Dunn
1743, March 6	Patrick Dowdall	Sophia Dowdall
1748, Dec. 7	David Morrison	Patrick Connelly
1749, Oct. 3	Thomas Barry	Robert Jackson
1752, Feby. 5	Nicholas Sullivan	Patrick Connelly
1763, July 4	Patrick Wayland	David Henning
1768, Sept. 5	Charles Conner	John Conner
1777, Nov. 20	Thomas Collins	Susannah Collins
1784, March 2	Mary O'Neal	Abram Simons
1791, Nov. 1	John Dempsey	Sarah Dempsey

From Deed Books of Spottsylvania County.

Parties to Deed.

Date.	From.	To.	Witnesses.
1722, July 8	Robert Smith	Alex. Spotswood	Joseph Delaney
1724, June 2	Henry Webber	Edwin Hickman.	Francis Conway
1726, Aug. 8	John Shelton	Aug. Smith	Edward Newgent
			Peter Kilgore
1726, July 6	Isaac Walters	Thomas Smith	John Kilgore
			William Muckleroy
1726, Jany. 31	James Brock	John Durret	William Logan
1728, Dec. 17	Alex. Spotswood	Thomas and Martha Byrne	Henry Collins
1729, Feby. 4	Edward Franklyn	Rice Curtis	Bartho. Mackdermot
1729, June 13	John Haddocks	Francis Thornton	John Prendergrass
			Francis Mecall
			Robert Green
1730, June 24	John Waller, Jr	John Waller, Sr.	Michael O'Neale
1730, Oct. 6	John Ashley	William Smith	Richard Gill and
			James McCullagh
1730, Oct. 6	Philip Brandegan	John Wells	John Dowd and
			Henry Collins
1730, Dec. 13	Edward Price	Charles Burges	Bryan Shannon and
			John Blake
1732, Feby. 4	William Taylor	Henry Elley	Charles Barrett
1733, April 3	Moses Battaley	Richard Tutt	William Kelley
1734, Jany. 28	Thomas Wright	William Hackney	James McDonald
1734, Feby. 4	John Rucker	Peter Rucker	Joseph Delaney
1733, March 5	William Bryan	Philip Boush	Henry Dongan
1733, March 11	William Crawford	Benjamin Coward	D. Byrne
1736, March 12	John Anderson	Robert Williamson	John Haley
1734, April 30	William Beverly	John Burke	———
1736, March 24	John Rogers	Abr. Rogers	William Conners and
			Walter Fitzgarrell
1737, Jany. 1	John Chew	Henry Martin	Michael Guarey and
			Patrick Dowdall
1742, May 31	Edmund Waller	Samuel Brown	Michael Lawless
1744, Oct. 2	William Lea	Anthony Garrett	John Coffey
1745, Oct. 1	Richard Todd	William Lynn	William Kelly and
			William Hughes
1746, March 3	Benj. Matthews	Joseph Carter	Thomas Magee
1747, Feby. 3	John Allan	John Mitchell	Patrick Mitchell
1748, Feby. 13	Henry Chew	Jane Chew	Patrick Carey
1749, Dec. 19	John Allan	Robert Duncasson	{ James Fleming, William McWilliams, William Lynn, Thomas McKie
1749, Jany. 15	Mark Wheeler	Joseph Carter	Patrick Kennedy
1750, Oct. 2	William Smither	William Waller	Thomas McNeill
1753, Nov. 5	John Holloday	Joseph Holloday	Abr. Sweney
1754, April 3	John Allen	Thomas Allen	{ Patrick Connelly, James Collins
1754, Sept. 9	John Callahan	Anthony Foote	John Collins
1755, June 3	Thomas James	Henry Field	Ann Kenny
1757, May 23	John Brumskitt	William McWilliams	Thos McClanahan
1761, March 15	Benjamin Davis	Benjamin Martin	Charles Lynch
1761, Oct. 31	John Graves	John Graves	James Mackgehee

Date.	From	To.	Witnesses.
1764, Sept 29	John and Ann Pitts	Paul McClary	Edward and John Collins
1764, Dec. 15	Anthony Strother	Charles Carter	John Kelley and James Mullins
1771, August 15	John McKenney	George Moore	———
1772, Sept. 28	William Fitzhugh	John Chew	Patrick Kennan
1774, March 13	Joseph Herndon	Charles Gordon	George McCormack
1775, Feby. 1	H Harford	John Dixon	Patrick Lenogan
1779, Feby. 9	Oliver Towles	Thomas Towles	B. Sullivan
1779, Sept 4	John Faulcover	Samuel Parllon	William Grady
1777, March 17	Francis Wisdom	Thomas Wisdom	Benjamin Quinn and Edward Collins
1781, July 19	James Callaghan	Tully Whithurst	———
1785, April 6	Thomas Swiney	Thomas Montague	———
1794, May 20	William Rent	Robert Pleasants	James McCormack
1791, March 4	Jesse Bowlin	Robert Scott	James McDonald, Michael McDonald, L. Grady
1792, June 26	Patrick Donally	Joshua Long	———
1792, March 2	Thomas Ball	John Keegan	Patrick Keegan
1797, March 10	Jonathan Clark	Zack. Shackleford	Thomas Branan
1797, July 1	Mrs. Kesia Coyle, James Coyle, Michael Coyle, Lucy Coyle, William Coyle	William Richards	John Bogan
1797, February 7	John Keegan	Francis Brook	———
1798, Jany. 29	Benjamin Massey	Burgess Sullivan	William Sullivan
1795, August 11	Joseph McCann and Elizabeth, his wife O'Neal McCann and Sarah, his wife	Edward Herndon	———

SOME INTERESTING NOTES ON WASHINGTON, D. C.

BY MICHAEL J. O'BRIEN.

What is now the capital city of the nation was known originally as Carrollsburg and Hamburg, the former having been named for Charles Carroll of Carrollton. It was a tract of 160 acres, the title to which was vested in Daniel Carroll, Henry Rozer and Notley Young, under a trust deed from Charles Carroll, dated November 2, 1770. This conveyance authorized the grantees to subdivide the tract into 268 lots and sell the same. The deed was recorded at the Court House in Marlborough, Md., on November 20, 1770 (Liber A A, No. 2, fol. 299). Immediately following this entry there is on record a large number of deeds from the above three grantees to different parties for lots in Carrollsburg, which the deeds recite having been "drawn by lottery." It was the custom in those days to dispose of property by lottery, which was ratified by duly recorded deeds, to the parties drawing the lots.

When Congress decided to remove from Philadelphia, the choice of a Federal Capital was left, by courtesy, to Washington, and by virtue of an Act of Congress of July 16, 1790, the President appointed Thomas Johnson and Daniel Carroll of Maryland and David Stuart of Virginia, commissioners for surveying the district selected as the permanent seat of government of the United States. An act of the Maryland legislature "concerning the Territory of Columbia and the City of Washington," passed in November, 1792, recited, in part, that "Notley Young, Daniel Carroll of Duddington and many others, proprietors of the greater part of the land hereinafter mentioned, came to an agreement whereby they have subjected their lands to be laid out in a city and have given up part to the United States," etc.

Among the owners of the lots at this time I find on record Dominick Lynch, W. Regan, Daniel Ragan, John McDade, Frederick Maley, William Magrath, P. McMahon, William Deakins, Henry McClary, Patrick Manual, Lawrence O'Neal, James Neill, Captain William Macgakin, Charles Carroll, Daniel Carroll, Mary Carroll, Elizabeth Carroll, Charles Carroll, Jr., Richard Conway, Stephen Moylan and John Casey. Dominick Lynch seems to have been one of the most extensive lot owners in Washington between 1793 and 1796. I believe this was the same Dominick Lynch, founder of the city of Rome, N. Y. He was a very wealthy merchant and philanthropist, and is also noted as the first to introduce Italian opera into the United States.

Daniel Carroll was a very prominent man in Washington at this time. He was born at Upper Marlboro, Md., and was more than sixty years old when he became a commissioner to locate the capital city, but on account of his age, he continued for only three years. His wealth, prudence and patriotism and the leading position of his brother, Bishop Carroll, and of the Carroll family at large, made him to the end of his days a man of much influence in the public counsels of Washington. The Carroll estates in the vicinity of Washington were known as New Troy, Duddington and Duddington Manor, and comprised 1,428 acres. East of Duddington was an estate owned by one Jeremiah Riley as early as 1757.

In 1792. an Irishman named James Dermott was an assistant in the academy at Alexandria, Va.   He gave up teaching to become an architect and Griffin tells us that it was in accordance with a design drawn up by Dermott in 1795 that the Federal City was laid out.   A plan had been drawn originally (in 1791) by a French engineer named L'Enfant, but was not accepted.   The records show that on March 4, 1792, Dermott was requested by Commissioners Carroll and Stuart to draw up a plan.   He did so and the same was approved by the commissioners and afterwards accepted by Congress.   Both the original plan of L'Enfant and the improved one by Dermott may still be seen at the Office of Public Buildings and Grounds at Washington.

One of the architects of the Capitol, who was also the architect of the "White House," was James Hoban.   He was a native of Kilkenny, Ireland, and was taught the profession of an architect at Dublin.   In 1780 he emigrated to Charleston, S. C., where he received employment on the public and private constructions of the place, and at the conception of the capital city, Henry Laurens gave Hoban a letter of recommendation to Washington. He drew the prize for the "President's Palace," as the White House was originally known, and was employed to construct it. which he did with such particularity, stability and speed that it was habitable in 1799.   It has been traditional in the Hoban family that President Washington took exception to the style and proportions of the building "as inviting criticism from severe Republicans," but that he gave up the point to the architect.

There were several architects of the Capitol, the third to be appointed being the James Hoban referred to, who was ordered on May 28, 1798, "to superintend the building of the Capitol" and to remove to the city, where he was to reside at the house occupied by his predecessor.   Hoban also built the first post office in Washington and many other public buildings. and reconstructed the White House in 1814, after it had been burned by the British. He died in 1831, a wealthy man. and was interred in the graveyard of St. Patrick's Church, but the remains were later removed to a cemetery near Bladensburg, Md.   He left an efficient posterity, two sons in the United States Navy, another a priest, and a fourth, James, who was United States attorney for the District of Columbia during the administration of President Polk.—
From various historical sketches of Washington, D. C.